AUTOBIOGRAPHY

AUTOBIOGRAPHY

MARGIAD EVANS

'On her dulcimer she played'

CALDER & BOYARS
LONDON

Originally published in 1943 and reprinted in 1952 by
Arthur Baker Ltd., London
This revised edition with
'Margiad Evans'. by P. J. Kavanagh
published in 1974 by
Calder and Boyars Ltd.,
18 Brewer Street, London W1R 4AS
ISBN 0 7145 0977 9

Printed in Great Britain by
Whitstable Litho, Straker Brothers Ltd.

CONTENTS

MARGIAD EVANS

by P. J. Kavanagh

The years work like a sieve. After enough of them have passed, the writers of previous generations fall through, even ones who were great in their day, and only the truly big ones remain. Or so it seems, tidily, until we notice smaller, awkwardly shaped and cussed talents that have stuck in the mesh, refusing to fall silent. This is good, it would be a poor world if there were only Masters.

I dislike the words 'major' and 'minor' applied to writers, although we know what we mean, because it suggests that minor writers are only major ones on a smaller scale, diluted, not quite the real thing. Whereas in every age there are those whose gifts make no pretence of being inclusive, who are not ambitious in that way at all, but who hurl themselves on some portion of their own experience devotedly, obsessionally, until almost by the sheer force and friction of the attempt, it glows, and stays warm for good. They give us a shock when we open one of their probably forgotten books; we see them, and hear a real voice. Such a writer is Margiad Evans.

She was born in Uxbridge in 1909 and as a young child moved to the neighbourhood of Ross-on-Wye in Herefordshire, a landscape that wound itself round her for the rest of her life. It made her, to be brutally brief, but so we may know the kind of work we are talking about, a 'nature' writer.

After a start as a book illustrator she began early as a novelist. *Country Dance* was published when she was twenty-three, then came *The Wooden Doctor*, *Turf and Stone*; and *Creed*, her last, came out when she was still only twenty-seven. They are torrential books with a hefty charge behind them, especially *Creed*—dark, passionate, but clear as water, each sentence placed coolly, like a pebble. They had considerable success, *The Wooden Doctor* went

i

into several editions, but they are now unobtainable even second-hand. Anyone who has copies must want to hang on to them. Whether any of these novels will survive depends on the above-mentioned time-sieve. Possibly *Creed* will; at least *Autobiography* now has a second life.

Perhaps it is the most appropriate introduction to the work of Margiad Evans, though not the easiest, because it is a distillation of what she felt most deeply, written first as a journal when she was in her late twenties and early thirties, and not originally intended for publication. Because she has no need to invent, or disguise, her innermost preoccupations are here nakedly set out.

It is an intense book, an unyielding stare at that part of her experience she knew to be the most important. It has to be taken in sips, or small bites. She regretted this, and spoke of it in a later book: 'What is wrong with *Autobiography* is the strain, the continuous effort to put into language what was a deeply relaxing experience. The lapsing into quietude which I failed to convey because it was words . . .' (*A Ray of Darkness*).

There *is* strain. *Autobiography* is certainly 'a continuous effort to put into language' the inexpressible, but 'fail to convey' it does not. Anyway, we shouldn't take authors' public criticism of their own work too seriously. Only they know the height of the standard they set themselves, and Evans was properly firm in defence of her work when the criticism came from anyone else.

I believe it is true that man suffers most from what he can't express; something he glimpses, or thinks he glimpses, at the margin of things. It's as though we've been born without an organ of perception that we need and which, oddly, we seem to retain a memory of once having possessed. Some writers appear to believe they lost it in their childhood and go looking for it there, in past worlds. But Margiad Evans is more interesting. She's still in the hunt, determined to catch it in the fields when she's hoeing beet, when she's doing the darning waiting for her husband, or lying on sacks on a warm hillside. It nearly always escapes her of course—there's great desperation in some of these pages—but she comes near it sometimes and it is then, not surprisingly, that she most nearly approaches silence. The fretting falls away and we get one-word entries: 'Today . . . ' Fortunately, she doesn't often 'lapse into quietude'. Perhaps a true nature diary would be a series of blank pages stained with rain and juices.

I would like to defend Margiad Evans from the charge of being a nature mystic. Partly because it is too limiting a phrase, and largely because a writer has no business to be a mystic at all, in his writing. He's concerned with the communicable in the ordinary coinage of speech, and Margiad Evans is the least abstract of writers. She was attracted to nature because it is not man-made and therefore, to man, surprising and informative. But her real subject is the problem of expressing *this minute* in Margiad Evans' life, not a memory of last minute; it is an attack on the way the immediate seems always to leak away between the words when you try to express it. She happened to be in the country but her subject would have been the same if she had been surrounded by traffic and pavements—because her subject was herself.

It is in this sense that her book justifies its title. In the ordinary autobiographical sense it gives us hardly any information at all. But of what it was like to be Margiad Evans, to live inside her skin, it tells us as nearly as possible everything.

Such successful communication is not achieved through good will and letting it all spill out. She was an artist, confident of her aim and method. 'I believe that the most lucent form of writing one's thoughts in earth (as distinct from thoughts in the brain) is in Notes or daily journals. It is most difficult and painful to rely on memory, which having its own tricks of colour and its own tastes, is always ready to substitute and reform . . . If I try I get a false picture, one from a collection of memories—something "typical" an academy "summer".' She regards her work as a form of bearing witness to her experience: 'I understand without words the thought that is in me: but without words what may be *testified?*' Sometimes she finds the effort almost unbearably difficult. 'Must I—must I begin again? Without any help? Each time I take hold of a pen it's like being born—and the spirit hangs back *knowing* the greater joy of unconsciousness.'

Consciousness was her duty.

'Helplessly poor (two glances at a penny sometimes, at the mercy of a shilling) *horribly* poor I am, but this is my chosen work, and as I scribble away here I do feel in harmony with a true purpose. There's the peace of contemplation and the peace of being in the fight . . . I've felt both today.'

She *was* in the fight, despite the fact her chosen work demanded solitude. It shouldn't be necessary to emphasise this but it probably is, because ours is not an age that over-values the contemplative virtues. Any withdrawal from our fellow creatures tends to be regarded as a retreat from reality, self-protective. But it was reality she doggedly pursued. Man is not only a social animal. Her search was to 'hear' what the natural world was 'saying' (the inverted commas are not finical, the verbs could mislead: more precisely, she wanted to show that natural forms were not 'saying' anything at all, they *are*, just as she *is*). She was making a single-minded attempt to establish a true connection between the human inside herself with the non-human outside, and this work has to be done alone.

She knew that her separation from others, while she was searching, made her appear odd. 'I live by intervals of peace, when nothing is spoken but all is comprehended. Or I would if I weren't recalled. And people want answering. Unless one is in a state of perpetual reciprocity they imagine one to be either mad or angry. One looks *out* suddenly and sees that, startled, they are waiting for a normal explanation of one's spiritual absence.'

The admission of spiritual absence might sound unattractive, it's as though we resent somebody preferring the company of roots and clouds to our own. But we can seriously neglect the non-human world, to our great impoverishment, and she brings us news of it. To approach the lives of grass and moss and birds she had to separate herself from our lives, even from her own. 'I don't wrap myself in solitude, I go naked in it. I discard my particularity, I discard myself.'

It would have been easier to pass the time chatting.

When she observed people she was as precise and unclouded as when she observed things. '"Ah, Ah, Ah" she sighs, looking at the familiar feet in elastic boots which she has just put to warm on the fender. And her glance says "A fine pair of feet for seventy. I wouldn't change 'em for a motor car." Her twist of hair is screwed up as tightly as if the frost had nipped it, and the blue shade of her nose is the dim colour of the meadows in the early morning.'

But it was the livingness of things, and her response, that were her true preoccupation in this book, so that it stands or falls on her observation and her expression. She banks entirely on description, there's no dialogue, no drama, the greatest event is the passage of a bird across a cloud; it is difficult, dangerous, and, in my opinion, she triumphs. She accurately conveys, and directly, sights, sounds, sensations; without whimsy or falsifying or fine, over-cadenced writing. There are perhaps five hundred words here in which she lets herself slip a little, pushes too hard, becomes hectic, in a book of a hundred times that number in which every sentence, for a less pure artist, would have been a trap and a temptation. She makes pictures and gives the inwardness of the picture also. 'I saw a man who lay down on the field and put his arm into a rabbit hole as into a sleeve. The roll he gave his shoulder, as though he would pull the earth over him, as a coat.' She describes tracks, after a night of snow. 'I never remember *realising* flight as I did when out in the field some distance from the hedge I looked down and saw the treble markings I had followed cease—just stop without flurry or fading as if some natural thought had lifted the bird out of the world. The lonely snow, and there being nothing after those prints. I despair of describing the effect, but it lay in that which was missing, rather than in that which was there. The human record was complete . . . Between those narrow scutted ruts made by the thrusting forth of a heavy foot not lifted but pushed forward over the earth, lay no space for guessing. The tracks were pickets, tying the maker to the peg and the peg was home. Just as far as his work lay from his fireside, the rope that was in the heel of every man, uncoiled over the fields without giving one unnecessary loop to freedom.'

I have seen some of her letters, generous in self-revelation. 'The poems are rather a mystery to me. I always forget what I've written as soon as it's done . . . Do please, for friendship's sake, let me know when they are to be broadcast . . . I shall listen agog for news of my mind.'

She projected an essay on Emily Brontë. 'I do not know any word I can use which will describe my feeling for her. It is not reverence, and it is harder than sympathy—it is something quite inhuman. It is towards Charlotte I feel human.' In another letter she says something which suggests *Autobiography* was an early step in a spiritual journey. 'I was trying to trace Emily Brontë's progress from nature mysticism through religious mysticism to what I call universal and ultimate mysticism—a progress which is not unique but which enrols her among the martyrs of belief with the distinction of being one of the very rare articulate ones.'

Perhaps the key to the distinctiveness of Margiad Evans' work lies in the phrase 'harder than sympathy'—and in the last sentence of what follows. 'I wanted to try to restore the balance between Emily Brontë and some other women writers which I feel has slipped too far on her side. The admiration her work evokes today is unbalanced, uncritical and *stupid*. She would have scorned it. I admire so much modern work. It has beauty and interest. What it lacks is passion.'

Her poetry is oddly less pictorial than her prose. With most writers it is the other way about. This late poem gives news of her mind.

The Forest

In this life where no-one lives as themselves
I found myself moving in a great Forest. All was shadow.
And I walked deeply:
no bird song shone, no footstep
made a quiet beat on the Forest drum.
In the lining of the leaves
no light was torn; above no face of sky
shaped by the parted boughs looked down on mine.
And I walked deeply
without laughter or fears. And I walked deeply.

Mind or spirit in me saw the still roots
as deep under the trees as their branches were high.
And I walked deeply,
singing in the double-depth Forest
which was visible and invisible;
happy in a way no human being should be happy
in silence, alone, and in shadow.
I was like the heart of a dead man
singing in the grave, to be buried forever.
And I walked deeply in the Forest, when suddenly
there was a stone man with fresh white honeysuckle
crowning its blindness; and its eyes were stone
without flinching. And I stopped, for here was the effigy
of my joy: holy stone and white scent
linked to me, sightless, until the bald eyes
glared into tears, and the tears fell over the face
flashing like harp-strings . . .
A wild ancient air poured out close by me.
And I wept deeply, nor sung for the leaves sung so loudly.
And I wept deeply. And I weep always.

In the early nineteen fifties she was afflicted, without warning, by epilepsy. She wrote some poems after that, of which 'The Forest' is one, and an account of the onset of her illness, *A Ray of Darkness*, which is interesting for its description of the creative process (and its possible connection with epilepsy) and remarkable for an astonishingly factual report of her first fit. She remembers what she did before, did after, and how she felt as the fit entered her mind. She is so precise and cool, and her behaviour afterwards is so practical, that someone remarked at the time what a marvellous murderess she would have made.

The discovery of her epilepsy, at the age of forty, coincided, more or less, with the birth of her first child.

After a time of hope, it became clear there was some damage to her brain and in 1958, not yet fifty, she died.

P. J. Kavanagh
1974

TO

MY HUSBAND

AUTOBIOGRAPHY

A LITTLE JOURNAL OF BEING ALONE

MIDWINTER and all dulled but the wind and the stars. The dead of the dark winter; stretching behind me the dim patch of silent days alone. The wind is a tooth in the breast . . . the dark suns give no light.

There was no sky—only the breathy air and a heaviness behind the trees like the dull butt of an iron bar. I watch the moribund chickens standing about on one leg with their claws crimped like a bunch of twigs. A draught that seemed to splinter the bones, ran an icy tune along the hedge and leapt with the wind, dragging after it the straws combed by the brambles out of this morning's load. In, in, shut everything in. Oh the happiness of being alone—it's like having only one door to yourself and that bolted and firm walls round. The taste of it is in my food, the sound in my footsteps. I enjoy it even when terrified of my own alarming presence in the welcoming void.

Down the orchard getting wood, I said, 'That's the smoke of my fire.' In a moment I shall light my last candle and go to bed. I'm going to sleep on my elbow and my shadow lurches over the page. There's a noise far away in the dark which seems to know where I am. Why do all such things recall Death?

. . . . . .

Poetry has a scent. That sounds finicky, but it is true. More and more I turn to the poets for my reading, yet my appetite is spare. A line sometimes lasts me for weeks.

I was watching the wind dabbing at a dead oak leaf, but my mind was full of the poets and their ways.

Wordsworth's verses *are* the earth; he was the poet who turned with thanks to his dear friend the earth. His poetry is

like the hill-side grass with here and there the bounding note
of the bird above it, turning, darting, scooping the air under
its wing. Burns was gnarled as a root, fluent as rock water,
strong as a gale. When I read his poems I feel the coldness of
his rugged hand, red from its scrub in the stream, flying over the
paper, stamping it with his visions of love, and garbled pauper
devils. Blake was an idiom. Byron cut his teeth on gall-stones.
Keats was the sea and Shelley the starlight so secure in the skies.

.   .   .   .   .   .

I love the alert freedom of being alone. Anything may come
and you are ready to grasp it.

When night-time bars me in
and I am sitting sewing
my fancy takes the whim
to think of snowdrops growing,

they sprinkle grudging places
with slender drops of white,
and hang their orphan faces
in narrow hoods of light.

So frail I must recall
The shoulder of the cloud,
the scratching of the squall,
the wind, the frost, the flood.

Child kindness of the year
Young promise of beguilement
more tender and more dear
than old fulfilment,

How strange it is to see
and hard to understand
your silver shine like charity
in winter's stubborn hand!

Happy no longer, but full of those horrible thoughts which one pushes off one's life only to find them round one's deathbed.

> Gwendolen feared
> all things that stared
> lips that jeered
> jaws that fleered
> moons that were weird.

> Gwendolen feared
> the whispering string
> that would not sing
> but told the music
> when to begin—
> that Gwendolen knew,
> yes, through and through.

A bird sang that. And 'Egypt, Egypt' sang another passionately. Their songs were so long this evening and smooth like psalms. And the air was like a church and the twilight lasted and lasted till it wore itself out on the wall. Like a door shutting. At last there was only a chink and a keyhole. The verger had gone home . . . the moon made me think of an insect as it crawled along the branch of the ash tree.

.   .   .   .

Thank God visibly for the day and the night which passed for me like one hour of contentment. Snow. It has been snowing all day without an interval in the silent bustle of flakes. There was a darkness behind the giddy pattern of the snow-dots; they fell past the open stable door, never colliding but drifting into a quiet little ridge on the stone step. And in the crooks of the trees were great lathers, soft and swollen as sleeping birds. There was so much movement with so little noise that I felt I had gone deaf. The only sounds were the farm dogs' rough 'Hew hough-hough,' and the splurge of a mass sliding from some woody ledge in the copse. The trees appeared to have put on flesh; their silence was softer than in frost time, with none of

9

that tense endurance of pain. And the dark grey sheep were in the white field. I felt rather than saw the subtle birds near the ground flirting from bush to bush. Such a lovely unconscious day. I never once remembered that there was such a person as myself and that I was there chopping and sawing logs, and gathering faggots and brushwood which had to be lifted from under the snow and beaten against the trees. The only assertion of existence was blood warmth and the feeling of beauty in the winter undertones of yellow and white and black and grey which made up the humanless landscape. Life ticked like a clock, fell like the snow, was folded like hands before the fire they built.

.   .   .   .

'And the moral of that?' I asked myself at the end of a long, long silence when I found that I had forgotten to do anything and everything was empty, burnt out and run down. Don't talk to me of morals. To draw a moral is to draw a bolt. One entertains one's imagination (or some one else's), makes a pretence of being friendly, and then suddenly bangs the door in its affronted face.

Oh the ruin of the snow! In the night the wind blew like ten thousand brass bands and strewed the countryside with splinters. Black and harried was my brain with internal confusion, injury and damage done while I was asleep.

I looked out. The clumsy snow was grey. The trees were groaning and squeaking and rubbing their branches irritably like men with lice under their skin. Where the wind touched the snow had slipped sideways and dissolved: the drowned earth loomed leerily, boggily full and repulsive. Pale fat carcase. I've seen dead sheep come down on flooded water which resemble those fields.

But ineffable sounds are in the sky. Another territory is above me; other beings cut off from the world fight and struggle in the cloud. *Peace*; that too came under the mallet of the gale. I heard the thud on its skull. Each day is spent in hard labour. I carry, I bear, I lift, I fight, not with angels but spadefuls of muck. My adversaries are wet, cold and hunger, my tempter is the fire. My sleep is a dog's. It's my life to dig and saw, cook and wash and gather sticks to warm my sleepy evenings. I know that I'm not great but small and that I'm not afraid.

.   .   .   .

Earth has come to itself again under the deft handling of the tender sky. Not exactly afraid, but conscious of my infinite solitude, I paused in the hall and for a moment thought vividly of the isolated moonlight round the house. In the mornings I shout at the dogs, sing, run loudly from room to room. But when it is dark I find myself hushing myself, walking in a whisper, as if afraid of letting something overhear my existence. . . .

I didn't draw the curtains after sunset and when I turned my head from the fire I was shocked to see the immense green light of the sky and its enormous even space bending the corners of the black earth outwards like the opening of a flower or the binding of a book held too near the heat: it broke the back of the hills: the small plot of the skylight held the same immensity of still, emotionless space as the whole: it seemed more fearful for there being no stars, sun or moon, nor any direction for the eye to cling to. How lovely Gregory Cock looked in the orchard on the green grass! Scarlet comb, gold and silver ruff, large feet in yellow boots, grey waistcoat. I ought to have called him Apollo.

.   .   .   .

The storm has wrought a queer privacy round the hill. All the telephone wires are down. The roads were too bad until yesterday for cars to get up the hill and the weather is still too cold for people to call. The silence is so impregnable that even my thoughts of people outside its line are small and hesitant. One lamp is going out.

I had a strange and fearful dream. I dreamed they killed me. The first shot missed and tore the skin off my knuckles. Blood ran. The second went through my heart. I heard my death shriek and died. Then waking in the curtained room I was alive again. I woke in the middle of a thrush's song. By its strong tone

I knew the snow had neither dismayed nor deceived the birds. Their voices throb like arteries. Winter is broken. But winter is dear to me. Come back.

. . . . .

The atmosphere to-night makes every sound separate. Some one not human is walking about the other end of the house. Old Mrs. Lloyd came to tea. That farm in Pembrokeshire years ago. Cutting off a pound or two of ham, fetching yourself a couple of eggs and carelessly skimming a cupful of cream. Martha, the housekeeper, the three scullery girls lying in one bed telling ghost stories. Then up in the morning very early to pull young carrots and scrape them at the well, and eat them before running down to the river where Mrs. Lloyd said you could see the trout swimming. Picnics on the ricks, the farmer thundering down below. Bread baked in the kittle, an iron pot with peat stacked round it and the smoke rising straight, in one huge loaf. Riding the cows home. The girl who kissed them on their noses and eyes. . . .

Now the old people dead and the young orange-farming in South Africa. At the farm, cars and machinery and no more maids walking up the hill late on a summer's evening to fetch the best water from the spring.

. . . . .

The gossip of the waters rushing off the hills is endless. It is like the hysteria of people running from disaster discussing it as they flee, and sometimes breaking out into a cackling revolutionary song.

. . . . .

What a sour thaw! As soon as you put your nose out it's wedged tight in a crack of wind. Faces show a brisk red, noses are kindled and features screwed into a grotesque likeness to those on Toby jugs and old glazed cider pots.

The slow funerals of old folk creep into the churchyards: knees are thrust into the fire, and people sitting thus are red in front and grey behind. The wind has blown shoals of oak leaves out of the wood and they lie there silvery brown, while from the scrubby shelter of a bush or a hedge rises the bitter wailing of a new-born lamb.

Ah, what a time for the year's remorseless nativity play to begin! A strange snow-gleaming light plays on it from the clouds. And sometimes there is another light—a light hard to describe—which seems to steal *upward* and be rounded off by trees and hills, a sort of window or thaw through the thickness of earth into a seasonless beauty, as though that spot were transparent over an ideal. I stare from the hillside up into the brown clouds where like dead leaves whirling, a flock of starlings is blown over the valley. The shouting crows rise from the grass at my approach and rush hoarsely into the air: in a moment they are hundreds of feet above the fields wagging their great disjointed wings like fins. The firs bend and let the wind out of the wood. A whey-faced primrose is a star among storms. 'Starvation's in the bed,' said Mrs. Lloyd as she hooked the kettle over a mass of fire. 'The days are opening and the weather tightening.' Now it is night. I hear the owls and when I pull back the curtain I see the moonlight all awry like the crooked frame of frost-bitten age. Cold, cold, cold. The stars amaze me. No one could believe such things of the day sky, that the clouded, hurried or one-coloured roof of daylight should turn into this utterly different possibility, this blackness all branched and antlered with white planets. It sends me cowering back behind my own eyelids, feeling my flesh a safety curtain between me and the eternal steel of the eternal will. Which star holds to-night's dream or yesterday's memory? I have fancied an unrecognizable change in my face to-day—a look which is not mine and which each feature belies while showing it. Forehead—no; eyes—no; no, no no. Perhaps in a co-existence I have died to-day, or grown old and the terrestrial shadow of my spacious twin has darkened in sympathy. I don't know, but the strangeness is there. Oh! Gwendolen the wild, whose eyes are the shining of a lamp on shut eyelids. Gwendolen, the groundless spirit of the heights. I brought you into life while I watched one leaf turn over. But I can't bring you to prove yourself aloud; and so like most of

13

my creations you move only in me and sing your song of
quickening waters to the wild air and the wind.

> Where waters quicken
> and rivers thicken
> Gwendolen is there.
> Darkness like thunder
> rocks split asunder
> Echoes are under
> Gwendolen the Fair.
> Gray fogs are rolling
> mountains are furling
> about thee Gwendolen,
> Gwendolen the Fair.
> Thou spirit boundless
> ethereal, groundless,
> ghostly and earthless
> child of the air!
> Winter winds blow thee
> Sunny rifts show thee
> the valleys below thee
> Gwendolen the Fair.
> Oh, then thou weepest
> hidest in the deepest
> cloud, and in keepest
> thy wildest despair!
> That no ear may borrow
> Gwendolen's sorrow,
> Gwendolen the Fair.

But her voice? That isn't there, it is what the wind is
to night and night to sleep; it is music spurting where the
finger presses.

> Shake down your dresses
> the finger presses

the furious harp.
Hark! Sharp!
the stony fountains
in giant mountains,
earth's white daughters
the musical waters
make the step rebound
in recoil of sound
as the rock head quivers
to tethered rivers.

Prose thought. Poetic thought. The snowdrops in the broken hedge, the primroses startling the vague shadows. The pony in his winter fur grazing the slope with the bright moon in the blue sky, the garden gate and the bay tree smelling of puddings. The wind blowing cold through the brain, the woodshed, the Swedish saw, the round logs with orange ends, Mother piling sticks.

Then the walk to the bus down the hill and the dusky little humpback's twilight salute, 'good-night,' his deformed scuffle, his insulting shadow. If only one could bring a barrow and cart away his back! Ah, it isn't fair, there's no wit in it. The dusk filling up the gaps in hedges, waiting by gate-posts and barns, thickening in the overgrown patches. The thin and glassy shadows of the early moonlight, the fire, the speech of wood burning, the sleeping dogs breathing, lamplight, bed. I half saw, half dreamed it all, vanishing slowly into night, slowly, tranquilly, disappearing into the darkness. All were *safe*. Not only the powerful and sensible trees, but each unconscious bud and weak flower. I could hardly believe that they were there out *alone*, once I myself was indoors. Yet they were: each in its day-time place securely and peacefully furled. How unlike us! Nature is not more cruel by dark than by day. For every owl there is a hawk. Of night we needn't be afraid, it would let us sleep as sacredly, as devotedly, as the plants; it is ourselves that make us sweat to think of the night mind of man with all the soul's witchcraft rampantly awake and crawling through the dew. So we have to pray 'guard us at night' when we might be as familiar with the moon as the sun.

· · · · · · ·

Candlemas Day. Throw all your candles and candlesticks away. Where the wind blows it will blow till May-day. It blew from the north-east, a shrivelling wind, starving man and beast, blighting the down of buds. I feel sick with it. Even the weighty demons on my chest are shaken.

Mr. Lloyd, old and proverbial, living by the sayings of his Adam-like progenitors, walks about like the father of the hills. Said he, rubbing the wind off his bristles with his shirt sleeve, 'Ah, un do lick your face a bit,' and Mrs. Lloyd comes in and sits by the fire grumbling soothingly like a pot simmering. When she lets her shawl go loose, the smell of ancient weather craft fills the air about her like dried herbs. 'Ah, Ah, Ah,' she sighs, looking at the familiar feet in elastic boots which she has just put to warm on the fender. And her glance says 'A fine pair of feet for seventy. I wouldn't change 'em for a motor car.' Her twist of hair is screwed up as tightly as if the frost had nipped it, and the blue shade of her nose is the dim colour of the meadows in the early mornings.

· · · · · · ·

Night. The windows look as if they had been dipped in black oil—frost is tight about us. The bird winks his chip of black eye as I reach up my chilblainy hands to cover him. Moonlight, corpse light, flower light. When I look I seem to have one mind in another world. A step would take me—where? To the land M—— craves, the place that isn't home, where songs are sung fresh and never sung again, where there is running and wildness and fleet water? Oh, where leads the white bloom on the winter branch? Where, and what is the note I overhear?

· · · · · · ·

Day. In the black wood the sun flashed white like a bird flying. An unseen bird made a noise of ringing iron somewhere in the deep chilling shade. Not another sound, but cling-clang, cling-clang low to the matted ground. All black, black depths and the brink of dangerous knowledge. The wind flashed at the tragic clouds and fell back into its own wild country.

Later

I said, 'Who can be that benighted person walking on the bank so fast alone?' It was my shadow in the moonlight like an impression in wax of my own ghost. The rays of the moon slit through the house.

Only poets *know*. What was it I wanted this morning? What? By the fire, with patches of silence and patches of wind and the hours stepping towards midnight, what was I going to write? I'm like a very old woman knuckling my hands in my lap and repeating forgotten deaths.

The sunlight threaded the trees with bluish threads; it wove whole skeletons of shadows within the branches until the golden bark and roundness of the limbs were less solid than the inner lacing. Body and soul the trees stood, and the light fell out of a sheer sky white at the rim, a dark blue hole above. But to-night the stars crackled and spat. The earth was firm, but the sky ruled it and where they met light cut darkness to the bone.

.   .   .   .

I see the great sky out of the window—huge reaches of transparent glow. And the dead leaves of clouds lying still.

The lonely sound the winter makes!

.   .   .   .

A person may be so used to living alone that another creature on a hilltop a mile away jostles him.

In feeling there are others with me; but in thought I am always alone. The warm rain ponderously falling, the wind in one tree, the pale and shadowy sky flapping as an unlatched door—it was not *I* that was lonely, but *they*.

I sat, or rather lay, on the hillside just when night and day were reckoning with each other. The sullenness of months was broken, and the birds were singing themselves to sleep. A horse stood loosely on the rough slope, drowsing, quarters to the house. The wet grass smelled of tiny herbs under me, the wind smelt of stars. I was so tired that my body seemed to sink into its grave under the turf: my hands ungrasped and the world fell through the lax fingers. No more resentment. No more passion or complaint, tears or justification. No more grief and pain and betrayal. Only joy. *Thou* Father knowest me. Beyond the hard conditions of our life and fate, speak for me to those few I love, as I love this place on earth and this earth of all thy worlds. God be between us all like the lovely air.

It was pure delight to lie there with my dear home winds coming over the tops of the elms and my own country lapping around its incomparable hills . . . to lie and rest and wonder whether real death can be so perfect.

.   .   .   .

Far away from me the long stilts of pale light struck down into the smoke of hill and wood. The clouds were lightning-edged and the fine fingers of the poplars grew through the field like a hand. The light fell on the farmstead walls where they rose from the roadsides rooted in weeds, and made them peaceful. Beautiful spring of spring, hardly to be seen or felt, when there is only one of each first thing—one flower, one lamb, one twig of sun—is passing, passing almost without recognition. The birds sing more often, and the maternal clouds are suckling the slopes to fuller green. The cries of the sheep fill all the corners of the fields. But still a wintriness lingers like the ghost of a wicked man keeping step with the moon when his bones are grass. . . .

The light is bursting. Shelley's yellow fire!

Suddenly it rained a silent cloud, and turning round I went into the house and listened to the breathing silence that falls between the yes of the light and the no of the dark.

THE WINTER JOURNAL

CHRISTMAS, 1939. Brookend. Now is the time to start a long, long task or else to sit in silence unwinding my sadness shade by shade.

That's what I would have done had I not *sold* this twilit day.

We walked together by the river. It was a dark yellow green, rooted to its rock. The cattle gloomed over the water. It was cold and we were tired. There were so many people, and I have ceased to say 'tell me.'

Here I am where I began The Widower two years ago, and where I hope to end it if this year doesn't break my heart. I will do everything just as I used: put the lamp on the kitchen table, bolt the back door.

. . . .

The jasmine is in bloom against the back scullery wall. It's a cold, clammy thaw. Went to the station about my luggage past the Brewery. The building threw the street into grey shadow . . . a street which is nearly always empty. It smelt malty, and there was a soft hiss of steam. Men were rolling barrels into the reverberating entries. . . . M—— came to tea. I met him in the road between the Vine Tree and the Vicarage, walking in his sandals.

We looked at Lear but he couldn't amuse. . . . Watched the fire's tendrils twining round the iron bar . . . the chimney all furred and black, M——'s features thrust into the light. Oh hopeless time!

Christmas is past. I will look out of the window across the pinched garden to the hill which seems more like a reminder of home than home itself. I cannot remember that I have lived there. The hills across Jones's field were a wintry grey, the lawn pallid with frost. In the apple trees many decayed and frosted apples—to me a strange dark red blur. The sky was ominous, the sun standing under a low entrance of cloud. At night moonlight, frost and fog.

.   .   .   .   .   .

To-day the church spire stood up in the faint atmosphere but a shade emphasized upon the air and the rest of the town was spilt pell-mell like a hasty sketch over an imperfect erasure. It was very beautiful—a momentary joy. To-morrow I unpack and start The Widower. Have done nothing to-day but knit and mope inwardly though outwardly only a little pale. But I pay little attention to my obsequious image. Asked M—— to write a diary.

.   .   .   .   .   .

The fire grows white with drifting paper ashes. A tiny yellow flame making a tiny noise. Now *why* at midnight should I be reminded of one of the grandest happiest prayers of thankfulness that I ever consciously uttered?

It wasn't a quiet day and not luminous, but wild and shot with keen gleams. I stood enraptured. Not a moment in earth or sky but was answered by my inmost spirit in perfect and audible praise to creation for its stern kindness, its harsh gifts, to me. I was nearly penniless, I had no near hope, but I had my senses to reflect the earth about me. There was a strange perspective, a light like wind, a nearness and a farness hard to define. The small horizon had white facets sharply cut which shot rays over the low dark fields . . . the minute trees in the distance, then the hugely disturbed branches over me—elm, oak, pine and ash clashing their naked arms while a vast flock of crows, black as demons and *separately* huge, drove over the road, low and hoarse as the wind itself. They were so large, blowing and flying, that the air was unbalanced, and rocked, while dizzy sight tried to take them in and the small remote skyline behind them. The fields grew less and less under the withdrawal of the clouds: the old lichen-dim woods crooned in the hollows and all around was the presence of the weather and the wind. I can see it now—the reddish hedges with their rusty stalks like wire, the hovels of hayricks, the cattle—and feel the delight filling me. Before it was over I looked to the west. The sunset

20

was lower than the most diminished tree, the earth sank before it in a visible curve, over which the night, seen like a dark cloud through sunshine, was rapidly falling.

Oh how long it is since I have looked at the greatness of nature miserably, through my own dreariness! *Now* it is my great refuge, my independent godliness which I worship without self-pity. It's a beautiful change from the tortured symbolism in which creation is molten and twisted into the form of *self*, to the simple and ever open sight of love! The fields are my grass life, the sun, the wind, the weather. If this power over my solitary hours persist, I am blessed.

. . . .

To-night a low roar like sinister machinery, like fire in the dark. The footsteps past. My hand cold. The whole town silent. . . . The yellow and brown bird singing, a red rose painted on his cage. I cannot in the stillness recollect his notes. Midnight and no more margin.

. . . .

I have put a mug of winter berries on the table and covered the birds with a newspaper. The fire burns brightly with a sound like twigs underfoot. M—— brought me to the door. Last night *the laughing nightmare*, very very horrible and terrifying. I woke laughing and kept sinking and waking again, choking with laughter and the sensation of hands brushing my throat. A flat light dim and undefined as moon vapour shone over the top of the curtain on the ceiling. In the morning *snow* and its reflection striking across to the pale green door. Looked out of the window. No sky, but solidity about the buildings and the trees blue. Snow stuck in the palings. A woman in the middle of the cross-roads standing and looking dazed with the shock of the change.

Shopped with M—— who brought me a letter. Went for a walk alone by the river. I saw, but about half-way seemed to lose my sight in meditation. The town behind me showed stark white squares and oblongs in a looming khaki mist. The berry trees a heavy red, the snow melting in little round pox, the grass piercing it like a needle through linen. The river repeated the density above it only more darkly. It was all silent save for some water birds whose feet scratched the surface with white weals as they rose. But the river brought thoughts of our childhood as it always does. I'll go to bed.

(Sometime early this morning before the light broke I heard a trivial bell ring twice, and I instantly saw under my eyelids a hand, impulsive, gross and autocratic, lying on a table near an invalid's bell, and trembling with anger. I saw the wrist and the frilled sleeve but not more. It was not a dream.)

December 29th. The sheep, wrapped in enormous foggy fleeces, swollen with lambs, were invisible to my eye until the mass of them began to run across the field, bucking over the tussocks. Their feet made a sort of papery rustling in the snow with a heavy throbbing underground. Tufts of grey rushes packed around with snow, crows, flatness, cold. . . . We went up Chase. Sat on a stile in the sun and stared at the snowy fields falling and fading into yellowish vapour. A line of ice-green in the sky was the only colour save the vivid dead gold of the oak leaves against the dim white landscape. . . . Went behind the hill along the little wriggling black paths between boulders under snow.

It has been a perfectly still day with sunshine like a faint gloss on certain slopes: but not enough to reveal the long mountains or to illuminate the sky. All had an undefined half obliterated beauty in which the trees looked like clouds and the birds were colourless. It was winter, silent winter. A dog barked and that was all. The midday thaw was freezing again and the fallen trees under the snow were sleeping forms.

We saw a ruined barn with humbled walls and bramble sprays thrust forth from a door of mossy planks still hinged on to the post. There was no breeze to jar it. The sun shone into the roofless oblong and out again by the slits in the walls. The stones were huge and green. As I looked back I saw it there behind us dark and fallen in the windless empty heath, with evening round it, and a confusion of cloud.

22

'You suit the woods,' M—— said. We lit a bracken fire and made a bed for Gladys. While the light lasted a pleased robin kept near us. He seemed to like us to be there. The sky turned a pale lilac with stars, and the branches stretched in hard, thin pencil. The fire began to give light. We might have been alone on a rock in the north. The sparks dazzled us and made the stars fade. Sometimes the dead bracken crisped under the frozen snow . . . a slight, dry stirring like an animal. Then darkness directly above the lightness and the disappearance of the air and the trees.

Returning the snow gave us a light to see the space below us, transparent to the deep still bottom. Our hill's back bore us, so that standing still we seemed afloat upon air, far above the black valleys. On the one side lay the shadow of the forest, on the other the silent luminous white plain of the river, phosphorescent under the vivid constellations, stretching out of sight to the foot of the Welsh mountains. Oh it awed us, not to *look* but to sound with our eyes so deep! Oh the loneliness, the silence! No tracks but ours, no voices but our own. Oh the mighty sense of the spread earth below us, the utterly pure night air we drank! The path ran by the elvish rocks which sometimes hid the stars. I forgot everything in the larger being, in the mysterious earth bared to the winter sky, in each star spaced and separate, intense and rare!

Down at last we separated. I was tired, and *then* I felt cold with the chill of the river. Lame and changed I went on alone in a quietness of shadows, along the polished road. I was dried up with thirst. I saw a light in a corner of the Vine Tree window, so I went in and drank a glass of cold sour cider. Only an old man warming knees like elbows in the wood blaze, and the Landlord and his wife. Home with sore feet. Finished a letter, finished the cigarettes. Finished the fire and wrote on my knees by the little footstool, to the droning of the waterfall.

Later. I am so cold. I crouch here like a stone over a grave and the room grows empty as the frozen ground, and the sun we saw goes under the world. Voices. When I'm indoors I cannot

get out of the darkness and fear. Indoors I'm so old—throw a
shawl over me, I'm dim. But when I'm out in the fields and see
the hills just as they were when I was a child—then I *am* a child
and I touch things and feel childish knowledge in my fingers.
If I had daily work in the open I should be so happy just to see
and hear. I'll ask M—— to let me help him with some sawing.

. . . .

At the table leaning on my elbow, looking out of the window.
A blur, a thaw. The canaries jumping. The only sound in the
room was their claws on the tin bottom of the cage—and then
suddenly a single *retroussé* bit of song like a jest from one of
them.

The divisions of time fail. As I sit here I don't know whether
it's to-day or yesterday, and I don't believe the rooks do either.
I seem to have a part in each and nothing to join them together
with. There's a memory in me like a landscape full of my first
delight. The larks are singing over a field and the white clouds
rise from the earth line and spread over the grey sky, and I ask
myself, 'What is it that's here?'

. . . .

This house soon warms up in the morning with good fires in
the kitchen and sitting-room. The birds are bathing in their
drinking water, the paper man has just been. Blue hat with a
feather in it. Saw the same crow fly past the same tree at the
same time—the tree a bluish brown stain, perfectly immobile,
the earth dark like saturated wood.

It froze again. Up the garden to pick groundsel for the
canaries—still snow along the garden wall and frozen in the ivy—
the cabbages, the path with frozen footprints, and no wind to
make the trees alive. Birds like mice creeping over the ground,
grey and small. I shall take Gladys out and carry a basket for
twigs. The sky has lifted. I see a soft scattering of cloud on the
yellow atmosphere.

Later. I gathered sticks by willows and by elms. The sun rode
low in a white mist, the hills were hidden, the fields flat white.
All at once, a change! the sun smiled on the uneven surface of

the snow, making thousands of blue dimples. A blue sky dotted with white cloud. In the east an immense white bank shaded to the misty horizon, its loftiest ridges smoothed with white so that all appeared like a bright pasture under an ice mountain. Peewits and crows on the wing. Blackbirds and thrushes surveying the flat of ground from the tops of the hedges. Flocks and flocks of dry bent brown leaves on the field.

Now the world in shadow while all clouds hasten to the sunset.

.   .   .   .

1940, *January*. Why is it that all my visions avoid me? I believe it is the darkness of the house—and oh the cold! For when I'm walking about upon the little paths among the bushes, my visions are there under my feet and they have words with them. But when I come in—oh I can't explain. I want words. More words for colour—for the blue which is beyond the grey sky; for another blue which the hills keep for days and which is *substantial* in a disappearing earth—and another word for haze or mist which is not dimness any more than the stars not shining in their nonentity. I want words which open, words for space, words which *will not bend the thought*. Is there such language? I believe there is. I believe I hear it. I aspire. Oh what do I not see in the sky and the earth. Thought rests on them like sight, and in harmony I think and see. This morning I went up Chase and sat on a tree stump. All below dim and yet sunshiny —the ploughed fields still white with snow, the farmhouses shining, one slate like a star. Up on the top there blew a silvery breeze. A pure blue green heaven all around and far below the valleys in the shadow of the hills!

To my journal. A beaming day. It never stopped freezing. The others went out to get wood. I stayed at home. The pleasure of closing shutters, stirring sleepy fires, lighting lamps. I looked out of the back door. It was perfectly still, icily cold. Brown smoke from the mill going straight up and then bending over like a broken feather. The sky exquisitely clear, fading and darkening to the town's dusk of smoke and shadow . . . the lid of the well was open and I saw the living water, square among the flag-stones. My hand was on the door-post. The water and the sky, the mystery of far and near.

This morning Chase seen whole against the blue. A shadow lay in it like that hollow under the bone of a thin cow. Rocks were sunny and woods a sunny bronze.

 . . . .

All day a fog of frost on the window with a bright patch of thaw just the shape of a snow boot. Saw the garden path through it. An apple branch on the kitchen fire. Birds sang. I heard the plovers. Last night I dreamed I was talking to a man and a woman who were about to be hanged. She had large, grateful eyes which have appeared to me distinctly in daylight. I can see them *at this moment*.

M—— cut down a laburnum by mistake. He had on his beret, his gum boots and his scarf and was standing in a mass of twigs. I had on my bedroom shoes.

We sat on the stump. The cabbages were like green and white rosettes. The snow and a little mimic tree rising out of it with a bird stretching its wing. Details too numerous and beautiful for description. All around subtle greys and browns and blues with the white to emphasize the old red brick. The town dull, and the sky covered and laden with cold. Last night was the hardest frost we have had.

We looked at a gull and then over the wall at the Quaker graveyard. The sloping wing of the cedar tree fanned slowly to and fro, the black ivy was crumpled under the snow, at the end of the path the iron gate stood ajar in a drift. By the other wall I saw something moving and made it out to be a large pale-brown bird bounding rather than hopping over the snow. Silent it leaped, and paused, and looked, without a sound, without a dead leaf's rustle, the solitary thing. Up and down it went, by the tall weeds and withered Michaelmas daisies, the length of the path and back, in a monotony of endurance. We ran to the house, brought back food and water and set them on the wall that it might escape the policeman's cat, and when we next looked it was pecking at the saucer. It was larger than a thrush. What bird can it have been?

M—— was looking at the faraway trees: 'they seem frozen to the sky.'

In the distance was no movement.

We had our tea together in the kitchen. The fire like a bundle of smoky rook's feathers, stirred in its iron nest. M—— shook the poker in it till the sparks fled up the chimney and the kindling drying on the oven caught flame.

At dusk the rim of the snow. . . .

.   .   .   .

Finished sawing the logs in the garden. Freezing—a dark clear ice on the roads. The little tree with rhyming branches left and right, clouds like surf. Oh the superb lift of the axe! it got right into me. . . . After dark I was out but I don't remember seeing moon, stars or hills.

On the 10th I went away. Gloucester, so low, a trail of grey architecture with niches of indescribable atmosphere and a burst of white smoke. The Cathedral, a trinity of wings in a pale pale sky. The dawning of midday and its waning.

And then the Cotswolds snowy in cloud, but quiet, without breathing. The woods upon them are sanctuaries for the desperate of those shadowless hills.

And now this horrible place, all frozen wire-netting and stone pavements. The buses run under the old rookeries, the elms are *trapped*. I asked myself one frosty afternoon as I walked along the allotments, how many feet which tread the concrete from general shop to doorstep, from doorstep to bus stop, had learned to walk on meadows? How many eyes behind those dressing-table mirrors longed for sights they might never see again— farms, stubble, the sky? It was a woman's face which made me fancy that the people here like the earth were country once, with country minds which look backwards to young light and joys strangely changed to age and weariness. The woman carried a basket on her arm. Her clothes weren't black, but they were somehow the very colours of regret. She was a widow perhaps with married children. Her lips were parted in her dim face. She looked full of care and worry, as if Death had sent her a message or two but she had not yet found a moment to examine or acknowledge them.

One street of the old village is left with the beautiful low church and the squatting gravestones in the grey grass. Old bones these villagers took to their graves—old married bones. This woman died in 1815, the year of Byron's marriage. When they placed this stone he was a young man *my* side of death.

.   .   .   .

Walked with R—— over the lock and by the river. Gradually my body warmed from cold to tepid, and from tepid to exhilaration. The flats very beautiful—brownish tinted rather than coloured, and now and again sunlit over the berry bushes and rushes. This river is silent and shining by the green banks. But everywhere the smear of houses in the distance and trains running. A lone engine drawing a void . . . one felt every inch was public and forsaken of the abstract spirit of nature and solitude. The smell of man, the heel of man, and at his heel, his dog on its Sunday walk.

But the colours seemed to breathe upon the soft brown air, so dimmed, so sun-redeemed the water. The quiet tall trees. The cloud of the weir. The green boat and the house on a reedy island.

January 8th. I listened—(oh God how I listened!) as I am listening now; *now* when I look at the door, *now* when I glance at the clock, *now* when I see the shadow of the kettle on the back of the fire-place. My hearing is stretched out to the poles, to the place where the sun went down: my ear-drums are taut, and yet this listening is to my listening then *nothing*, even though my senses are sweating. I listened and I heard a low swell of sound in the night. I heard sound before it is born and after it is immortal. I heard the earth breeding, I heard the stones sleeping. Oh how to say what I heard! It was wordlessly wonderfully beautiful and quiet as the hum of hibernating woods, even, **endless** and unstressed. I'll write no more of it—how should I

translate it? I slept and woke to the usual world. But I remember
something that I cannot renew—something that is remote yet
ever near and everlasting.

That was on my last night.

January 11th. Came back. We passed the new moon and the
evening star in a green, transparent, perfectly clear sky. The
star was in the bay of the moon. I felt we were crossing the
north.

In bed I heard the waterfall and separated the two different
kinds of sound it makes—the overnote which has a scudding
fleeting sting, like spray, and the thick spasmodic thud which
is the body of the water crashing into the pool.

13th. After we had posted the letters we walked down to the
river. The air was thick, white, frigid, the town a feeble shadow.
Everything was grey or white except one orange spray of cloud
in the zenith. Reflected *through* the grey-green ice it was a dull,
yellowy pool in the middle of the river. The gull which always
seems near to M——— was flying over the hawthorns.

How beautiful the frozen river was, though it made me
clench my teeth and hold my breath to look at it! Beneath the
white-topped bank lay a motionless reflection of a deep slatey
grey. Ice ran out on either side, its edges rustling with movement while faint mysterious noises broke on the silence—
crackings, gentle whispers and hisses as the floating ice was
swept down to touch and adhere to the mass which was formed
by the current into millions of round rigid whirls. The plate
of ice was composed of welded scales each with its rim of
stiffened froth. It tinkled and heaved as if loath to stick to the
half-sunken ice jutting from the bank. We saw transparent
pieces like broken glass floating down, fins above the surface.
And going farther along the bank we saw stretching far out
under the water whole floors of ice of a wonderful cold colour
—not grey, not green, but lighter than the water so that we could
see the edges broken straight off and tell of the collapse.

Near the edge the shallow streams and currents had frozen
into writhing strands like the thread glass in marbles. It was

the grey glacial hair of the ice maid, and she lay with her deathly cheek on her hand, willing the ice to form.

Oh there was a numbness on the earth and a pinching of cold about the shrivelling trees! The ground was compressed iron— a slab that jingled the bones in our bodies as we ran. And yet the distances were fading, and no line of sky was to be seen— no bright adamant frost-ring about the earth. The cold was disguised in a soft misty mingling of shades, of pale, tall trees and white air, still until you roused it by your own motion. Then you felt its bite on your skin.

No swans, no birds, no cattle. And no sound but the ice rustling and the cries of some boys sliding on a leaden gash in the snow, under the steeple. The sternness of Nature had chidden all creatures to cover.

Later. The hills have been removed. I haven't seen them for days. Somewhere they are hidden near me; somewhere there are strong sleepers bound by a freezing dream.

13*th*, *Sunday*. M—— cut down the ash tree. He came with the big axe—walked back about eight—a very dark cold night with a black mist and frost. I let him out, bolting the door after him. Paused in the passage with the image of the snow in my mind before going back into the warm room.

In the afternoon we went down to the river and looked with rare pleasure at the strengthening ice. When it was dark sat in the kitchen—the black fire-place and sooty chimney full of golden darkness, of wood flame. Pots and kettles singing. I stayed up till midnight for silence to finish what it had begun. Watched all the fires fall.

.   .   .   .

The depths of night reached. How the river creeps round the wide white fields! How shall I warm my bed? When I draw my breath the sheet is sucked against my teeth, my feet chatter together, my hair lies cold on the pillow. . . .

No letters for me. Barley soup at midday—colder than ever. Potatoes baking in the ashes. I mustn't forget to turn them.

Light flung over the houses. I drew my curtains back before

going to sleep last night and this morning when the sun rose it
touched the room with thick gold streaks like lamplight.

    .   .   .   .

Black trees, white sloping fields, the shadow of frost. I walked
about. Walked up Chase with M——. Between us and the
clouds, something silent. We looked down and saw the mighty
sunset filling the valley with turbulent vapour. Home again in
the dusk along the snow-blotched path. A sheep was lying down
on the roadside and standing over her was a red-cheeked cheerful
whistling boy. I asked was she ill? 'Oh she has had two lambs
to-day and now she can't walk.' 'Will they carry her away?'
'Yes, sometime . . . soon, Ted y'eered un say.'

Poor ewe brought down by bearing twins in the bitter cold!
I walked on and presently was passed by a whooping crew of
children all running to look at the 'yowe' in the snow.

The world seems congealing to stone—a round adamant ball
that chips the foot. At sundown world and round sun balance
each other across a pale void. Colour there is not: only a variety
of depths of blue and black and creamy white—except for a
strange infinitely pale green shade in the sky—a lake too faint
to outline. A single star. In the silent air is no motion of life,
no flight, no call. But like the skipping of dead leaves the birds
hop over the ground and rustle in the withered weeds.

And I'm glad to be home, for the river is frozen and in all
my life I have never seen the strange river in such fantasy. For
years and years I have watched its curled current sweep past
the bends and now that impetus is tied, is knotted and bound
within itself. Often I go and stand by it to marvel at the wonder-
whirls of the steadily strengthening ice. Once a blizzard swept
down with a hissing and a burning cold, driving among the
brown bushes. The thongs of the wind are tufted with snow-
flakes—they fell like a whip and a caress among the branches.
And then the fine snow rose in drifts on the surface of the river
and blew like a spirit expanding over the ice, and small birds
flitted from the crested willows with weird cries.

There are black holes where the gulls crowd and long black

even stretches of water between the empty, bleached banks, and the dull reflection of the sunset on the ice, keeping pace with me as I walk. The sheeps' wool hangs in the barbed-wire all thickened with rime, and the flat dry reeds lie in a ditch rigid under a welding of frozen snow.

About some heifers feeding at a trough is a sort of thaw in the air and earth—a softness of atmosphere almost like summer sunlight. It is a mingling of their breath and the colour given off by their deep red hides, and the dust from the trampled hay which looks so golden in contrast to the neutrality of all the rest. It was very beautiful to look at—warming to the eye.

Everywhere the leafless, scentless frost flower is blooming. It lies rayed on the ice; it blurs the blade of grass, it doubles the thickness of the boughs: when the snow came first it was as a casual flick, then a powdering on M——'s hair, then as a furious sweep out of darkness which could be heard alighting on the brambles and trees. And in and among it the dead river lay with the wind screaming out of a vortex over its blind unrecognizing face . . . to lie when it was finished utterly still and white.

I keep my water in a jug in the cupboard next to the chimney and I sleep as thickly dressed as I walk. When I go out I see the children swarming on the ice under the shadow of the town with waving arms struggling through the heavy light.

.   .   .   .

More snow. The sky is overcast and unrelieved. Atoms drift past my window.

20 *Jan.* M—— and I went out into an orchard. The snow was lying on the ground. Nobody had been there since it had fallen. It was very silent there among the old black apple trees. The tracks of birds and rabbits going to their burrows—the pricked snow under the trees.

21 *Jan.* A terribly hard frost. Everything glued and fast.

After hearing some spirituals last night I went to bed. My brain *quaked* with dreams. First I had finished my book and I knew it was beneath scorn bad—and then I was rattling about in a town bus. I came to the stop and got out by some windows like glass tanks behind which were dishevelled dummies. It was a clothes emporium and I wandered through endless departments where girls were folding piles of dresses.

'What are these?' I asked.

'Oh these aren't new,' they told me, and I roamed on.

'Where is the jumper department?'

'Up at the very top, madam.' So I went up a tight green staircase in the corner, my bag under my arm. And there was a little room with a window showing only the sky. A huge fat negress in turban and curtain rings with a skin like black puddings, was on her hands and knees blowing a feather along the floor.

'Have you any jumpers to show me?' I said.

But she didn't answer, so I knew she was getting ready for the children. Up still higher I went into ever dwindling empty rooms, until at last, toiling, I saw the sea! It was shining against mud islands and dull clouds and it was a strange, very pale, milky green. So then I found myself on earth again and there was the little boy I had known for years waiting for me. He touched my arm: 'Father is taking us to the lighthouse.'

I suddenly looked to the right and saw a soaring pale stone lighthouse and beyond it the sea bursting into enormous columns of spinning water. 'What are those?' I asked the little boy. 'Those are . . . those are . . .' he smiled and gasped: 'the dissipations!'

January 26th. Must I—must I begin again? without any help? Each time I take hold of a pen it's like being born—and the spirit hangs back *knowing* the greater joy of unconsciousness.

Even while I was ill I felt the guiltiness of the infant to be still-born who will not enter the struggle. All the time I was evading myself. I won't spend my days cooking and cleaning. I'll go and live in the woods. Oh no. You know we won't, don't you, Arabella? You know it will always be you. No faith except in the eternal *one*.

. . . .

Dreamed Dad's ghost was on the other side of the door. The candlelight—the hill—the red-haired young man, *one of my people*.

Dreamed of walking along a mossy path between the smooth

green trunks of ash trees. The cottage door was open . . . the room, the silvery light by the window, but the floor all darkness and the pressure of the low ceiling . . . the pattern of the mat fading into the corners, the kettle boiling on two red coals.

She was a little girl in a pinafore threading glass beads shaped like crystal beans.

29 *Jan*. The wind straining, straining as if it were trying to pull something to the door over the snow.

I'm like a fossil in the grip of a pair of pincers.

Burnt my writing. Makeshift. Pour passer le temps. And then to die as I suddenly believed, for ever.

I went out. I walked by the river. The night before there had been a heavy fall of dry snow and the sky was as white as the ground. Just houses and trees and the whiteness, and the very dark wooden figures of people bolt upright in the snow.

And all the time I saw my pen with its dried nib lying across the pile of MS. I felt my slavery, my ignominy, my dependence, my pauperhood. I could hardly pull my feet along. In my heart I wanted to catch hold of the walls and fences and lean against the trees. I seemed to be going towards the dark house, the house of Nothing. The clocks. The wind. The waterfall. I was ill when the river broke up. Now it was in spate, red, with balls of pale brown and pink snow driven under the banks and livid froth racing the current underneath. In bed I heard the rending of the ice. Now I saw hunks of it, grey, semi-transparent like soda, smothered in snow, crouching above the water. It looked colossally obdurate. My heart beat with sudden joy. Gulls were calling and crossing, shrieking and dropping. Ruddy and sure, as an arm that fears no repulse, the river hugged its white lands. It had risen and fallen, had smeared itself over the willows and left them full of scurf and rubbish. Grasses, sticks, dredge were stuck through them like hairs in a comb.

I stood there kicking the snow. There was none of that light which you cannot enclose in a line—that which is the *soul* of the eye and not the medium of sight. No, but just day as much in the ground as the sky. The sun wasn't visible nor the sun's house. Against a white wall the trees were shivering: their branches, rigid with ice, rustled like tinfoil. One dark evergreen was beautifully solid.

30 *Jan.* For several days I've been reading *Robinson Crusoe.* Oh lovely island, the voice singing oh Paradise! I am there by the illustrious sea—pale blue-green, warm, thin as a shell where its wedge is driven into the shore. How could he ever leave it? No other book has such a permanent and abiding home to offer to the imagination. I was there before Crusoe. I am the native of that desert island. Having been kept in more or less this last week I have lived there, have led a calm practical existence with saw and spade.

It's queer how the day runs down by itself. The snow is solid, the whiteness like paint. There are ledges of it in the windows.

One day when it was raining I went up the garden to hear the birds sing. Just for that and for a rest. Everything was veined and spotted with water—the branches tender and delicate shoots budded with drops, the ground and sky shadowy. I walked up and down the path but after a few moments *something* turned me back, *something* called for me.

Every time I come down the path and pull the door to and turn the corner into the passage I hope to see *something* everlasting. That is the faith in me.

I do so want to see living things as they are when I'm not by . . . a colour, a change, a man perhaps moving with the earth, in it, of it, wholly engrossed, and *alone* . . . perhaps an animal which doesn't see me, running and nibbling without fear.

It doesn't take a great force of will to imagine oneself non-existent, as one goes along observing without interpreting or composing what one sees. But if one is perceived there is nothing to recognize—only a recoil, and then the unconsciousness is broken, the separateness smashed by the retreat. I don't quite understand what it is I'm trying to write and in a week I shall know still less, but to be mankind is to see other kind fleeing. We have this perpetual rear and running view of a flawed creation.

I would see as the light sees. I would know as the earth knows

35

when it feels the grass pulled by the sheep, when it rounds the rabbit's nest, when the blow of the hoof shoots to its heart. I would feel as the water feels round the rocks and the roots and the breasts of the swans. It seems to me that there must be a feeling of touch along the horizon and the meeting of the clouds must mean sensation.

When the rivers flow, when the twigs move over the sky, when the wind touches the skin of the water, you can see the sensations they bring to one another, and your own body reflects them.

It happened when I was walking along the river bank one very cold day, that I saw beyond the verge of the ice, and under the alder branches, two swans and their cygnets. They were as if joined to the hard, dark water. And they didn't see me or hear my footsteps. There they were, strung across the river, their lovely *evasive* bodies modelled by the touch of the water, their heads looking down into it, meditating downward, like snowdrops into the January earth. They uttered no sound, nor breathed a movement. And in looking at them my senses were held between the edges of the dark waters as between blades, and my all being was calm, as theirs.

And again the same day I saw a man who lay down on the field and put his arm into a rabbit hole as into a sleeve. The roll he gave his shoulder as though he would pull the earth over him, as a coat.

One invents moods. But not that time. One never could invent the joy which wells up and floods over all the hard points—the submerging.

. . . . . .

It's five o'clock. The lamplight falls on this page—the window is pale blue with snow and sky, the earth a dark wall. The rumbling machinery of a horse and wagon goes over the pounded snow. This afternoon the sunset on the rough ice, chopped red, and the black edges of the glassy rectangles sticking out of the snow. The eastern sky was a pale frozen green with the light of the moon wrapped in it, and the stillness and the snow dusk.

. . . . . .

January 31st. Walked to V—— and back. The kitchen without

a lamp, grey, getting dusk, lit by the snow: the sense of size and the table like a plateau. As I left the evening was falling but the stare of the snow seemed spreading farther and farther. A white cloud was hiding Chase, the road a road to Eternity.

Heard the first lambs from behind a holly clump. Also from the cursed farm where horses and cattle were stabled in a shaggy dusk. Gladys ran along without a lead as no traffic was out. Home by snow light.

I got my own tea and ate it in the kitchen alone—cold bacon and bread, a piece of cake, strawberry jam. And here I am, still solitary, having found myself. There are blue flames feeding on a log; the kettles throw shadows up the back of the chimney. Very minute things are happening in this room: dust stirring by the backdoor, a fly on the mat climbing over a thread of cotton, a bit of gauzy black substance balancing on a draught in the flue.

February 2nd. All at once quickly, quickly, the Genie is here, the pen, the moment! And then again—gone!—it's too late, too late, he's gone.

A day, any day—the way I think it and the way I live it. Keep it like that. Body and spirit. I am thinking of the Professor to-night. Queer, queer. I haven't written a word and yet suddenly as I raised the cup to carry it upstairs, my hand trembled to write. And in the space of seconds while I took it up to her (the cup in one hand, the lamp in the other) I wrote *worlds.* It was strange the passionate desire stirring in me.

The dark to-night was a huge, a fighting dark. I wasn't happy going past the churchyard where the snow lay in dim ribbons on the walls and the clock was striking six. It seemed as if all *my* clocks had run down. My heart was like a ball of string unwinding in my breast and somebody was pulling at the other end. It jumped in my ribs and was getting smaller and smaller.

It is of course late. I always rest by the ashes. Last night it froze again and the snow is still here. And the fields are white, and the hedges carry thatchings of snow which shadow the whiteness underneath, like eaves. But the hills were there. Chase was a light but strong line; below that was a ghostly zone, then soft brown brush. I stumbled along setting my feet in other grey, glassy footprints which were moulded in the snow. The sky was not pure white as it has been, but tinged with a livid earthiness and indistinct vapour. The birds dropped down it silently like slowly whirling leaves. It was saddening all of it . . . winter touching the dead things.

Later. The hollies' beautiful black masses deciding space and distance. The outer hills and trees a bluish-brown behind white. The poplars pale and quiet: the dark pines groaning.

The oak tree, full of golden leaves and sky, stood by itself in the silent stretch of fields. It made the only sound—a rustling fall like a flock of starlings diving, or like straw being littered from a pitchfork . . . and it kept it all within itself, spreading nothing. Behind it was a snowy bank with lambs running on it. . . . I shut my eyes and listened, and saw it *in me* packed tight with dry, rolled leaves. All the other trees were still with twigs and branches frozen to the air. Black wood stuck out of the snow, and the wind came low over it, 'hooing' and squeezing through the hedge. A few sheep had broken through and stood on buried legs, bewildered in their snow-bound souls, not knowing whether to turn up or down the road. There was a blackbird in the ditch; but the oak tree and the indescribably grim note of the wind were the only sounds.

．　　．　　．　　．　　．　　．　　．

Pale hills, dark sky, dead trees, white fields. Tree trunks like logs. People like posts. The sky aground, no birds soar, no fire burns, under the snow.

3 . . . people spoke to me; but I heard them through a kind of preoccupation. M—— came and sat with me. At midnight I read *The Green Linnet* in bed. All the evening I was aching. Then I went into the kitchen to be alone when it got dark. The fire was glowing hot through the bars, the white cloth hung on the door, the water pan was covered to keep it from freezing. And I sat down wearily. To-day has been like some one else's dream. I used to think I could never become in the slightest degree insane. But now I wonder, if when I am a little older

and more homeless in my mind I shan't be . . . not mad, but . . . open? I find myself pondering, looking at my hands, my fingers, my nails, smoothing and twisting my hair, watching the shadows. Once I thought I saw a creature like a dead dog huddled in a corner against the water pan. It looked stale and stiff, was cindery and ashen-chested, had teeth—dead teeth. And it didn't worry me whether it was or was not there.

Later. It's a terrible thought that this time next month M—— may be gone.

4, *Sunday.* Oh so sad. The church bells gamboling inside out over the roofs. The big bell. In time it was all one heard, the death bell in the peal, the heavy tongued. I sat by myself in the kitchen with Congreve on my knees. Didn't read, or read without sense.

Winter is finished and its scenery sliding to ruin. White snow is brown water, only white again where the waterfall thrashes it. Rough streams rush past their banks under the green trunks of trees. Beneath the grass the sodden hills are draining into the river. The earth strikes the eye with its darkness and reality after the false light of the snow. A reeking fog sticks to the chimney pots: the kitchen window shows a row of raindrops: the townspeople are not the incisive shapes they were a week ago.

All is soft—rotten—clinging.

And I dreamed my hair was grey.

Oh now for the first green, young green pushing pushing through the black wet crumbs of soil, and a wind big with spring! And the release of light—oh light, to my heart and eyes!

I turn my head to the fire. There's a draught in my veins chilling all my body's passages. A black and coaly fire it is with short flames in tufts among the crevices, like crocuses in a rockery. A greeny smoke lights up the bulging bellies of kettles and saucepans . . . the shadows are a den of rocks.

6. The town. The different shelves of houses, like a damp store cupboard.

9. Lost count, lost everything. The world and life dark. I plod

on. The only glimmer the page I am writing—the only thing in existence.

And yet how often I am *not* writing—hovering.

'Begin, begin,' a voice cries in my ear . . . the voice that haunts me in the streets, speaks by my bedside, and goes with me into the hilltop. Ah if they knew what I hear!

Begin. I hear and I dare.

What a glorious moment when I made myself pretend that it is a great, rare book I am making! I forgot . . . the anger . . . that had driven me out. I forgot to be harassed and anxious . . . even that I was thirty-one, and being kept . . . in the power of others. I forgot in that moment *all* the human consequences. There must have been a strange look on my face, for I believed in myself, and the rest seemed lies.

I mustn't do that again. It's like stealing, like lies. It's drugging, and when the relief is past, is worse, for somehow one has robbed oneself of strength.

I think as I hear people in their rooms (old people), knitting, sewing, making up their fires, listening to the wireless—now they have come after all to the sitting part of life, and can't understand, or have forgotten, the harshness of the poor beginning.

Helplessly poor (two glances at a penny sometimes, at the mercy of a shilling), *horribly* poor I am: but this is my chosen work, and as I scribble away here I do feel in harmony with a true purpose. There's the peace of contemplation and the peace of being in the fight, . . . I've felt both to-day.

With M—— into the fields. The hedges were broken and purple. Particularly noticed the elder—naked-coloured stems budding in rings from the stem joints. The blackberry leaves all dry and dishevelled, purple and silver, red and dun. Another elder bush growing by itself, the stems being a most vivid green from a sort of mould or moss which grew also on a pig's cot nearby. Cocks and hens . . . lovely white hen and *le coq d'or* and the pony with a rat's tail. . . .

12, *Sunday*. With M—— over the hills and down among

their cracks—over the sunlight and into the shade of the woods. We were so happy!

> Take my soul to Paradise
> in February harmonies.
> And some old and dove-worn tree,
> bud-tinted, be eternity.

When I came back my hands smelled of the fire we had lit; my mind was clear and fresh and pure. I couldn't read and blur the remembrance with print. I sat down by the kitchen table, and again I went through meadows of thought.

Eternity? What's eternity? Time in heaven? Oh the drowsy dusk of mist and hill and night, the strayed glimmerings at the very end of day, the last rakings of light scattered over the path, the pale dead grasses, wan leaves and water, starless sky and edgeless hour!

We were out all day—took our dinner in a basket. Potatoes to bake, soup in a tin, sherry, oranges, cake. My eyes were gathering everything. For this is my beloved little season—the dawn, the germ, the winter-spring, so exquisite, so subtle and so short! It lives almost unrecognized: a hope, a search, a rarity. When you see it, it is gone: when you feel it, beware of its going: when you know it is there, it is over. The hills were brown as burrs, the rocks padded with moss. Soft, small clouds packed the sky. In the woods the white scar of the axe, the uncanny openness where has been closest secrecy. And silence. Such silence! You could hear the thoughts in your head rustle.

The hazels were budding with tiniest leaf, like beads. The old dry ropes of honeysuckle had broken into green upon the bushes. The broody yew was there hanging its heavy shade over the red ground. And everywhere the drifts of dead oak leaves, the pale dried plants, the wisps and rotten boughs, the thorns and knots and grey stems of the winter woods.

We made our fire on a path. It was slow and damp; the leaves and grass that we threw on it flared and went out in bitter smoke.

But we roasted our potatoes, and knocking holes in the tin, boiled and drank the soup.

It was lovely. I lay back on the bank and looked up at the rigging of the wood crowded into the sky. The smoke went up among the branches and made them quiver; but there was no breeze or movement, nor any sound except the sheep coughing, and the curlews. It was all entirely solitary, wild and far as the grey islands.

We were encamped at the very edge of the wood, on a bank. Through the slender trunks the mass of the hill was visible, darkening hour by hour across the narrow meadow vale. A single twine of ivy bound some of the saplings, the leaves black against the light. The trees were mostly ash, hazel and oak. Once late in the day a man called to me to be careful with the fire. That was the only voice we heard all day except our own. The changes in the light were like the changes in thought— shades, but not shadows. There was a ground softness dimmer than mist, a lingering on the dead leaves . . . pale, still . . . and then the vista of the twilight going farther and farther away. Waves of red firelight lapped against the dark. The wood pulsed. Day, fading, lengthened the line of the hill, and darkness seemed to bring it closer. The cuts and scratches that we got scrambling down its side began to itch and burn. Desert wastes lay outside the smoky ring of our firelight. Great starless silences, the lonely hulks of hills, the speechless spirit of night, earth and water.

13. To-night the waterfall sounds as if it had turned to sleet.

14. In a sad, quiet mood of resignation. A lovely sky which seemed as if it would melt into sunlight. And so, for a few minutes it did, and I saw my shadow on the golden field. The river was broad and green and singing, reflecting trees and sky . . . the meadows pale with wandering green paths, and millions of dry embalmed leaves. Seagulls, smoke . . .

Twenty past five, Valentine's Day, in the kitchen. A dark light coming through the window, almost a summer stillness.

Later. Those gleaming moments! It was the kind of sunshine, thin, sweet, that penetrates the leafless hedges by a lane and shows the little black-green ivy leaves, the bristles of dead stick, and *white violets*. I suddenly saw this.

15. Always when I'm down in the river meadows with the low blue trees in the distance and the flat ground stretching away, I hear the town clock striking three. I am carrying a basket of sticks. I pause. And the clock pauses between the chimes and the striking of the hour . . . a long, level moment . . . then the strokes, resignation, patience, solitude.

The sky is pale. The town is pale. Even the red brick is pale as red can be without a shade of pink. When I was younger I should have tried to paint it, or at least thought how beautifully I could have painted it. I saw a pair of swans and their water shadows. And then another. One willow swan. But the willows were ugly after the flood like crones in dirty fringed shawls. Bottles, silt, rubbish, left on the grass.

16. Engines hissing. The wind blowing through the palings. The brazier. That was to-day, walking along the path from the station between the water and the fence.

17. Awake for hours. Shallow snow, *a dark white sky*. Stillness in the faces of the houses. An invisible wind.

M—— came for a walk. We went by the river. The snow was virgin with only a few pathetic bird tracks. I was so cold we had to turn back. No sun; but a lovely still day with trees like the engravings on an old silver coin. Behind them the low tone of distance. Happy, happy, frail and far. Children's footprints.

Later. Went up after tea to ask about work at the factory. Moonlight and bright silence. The night went up the hill with stars.

In the town doors were opening and letting men out into the street. Houses all dark—chinking of keys. From the corner shadows people emerging and walking across the light. They appeared and went . . . a soldier in a greatcoat whistling.

When I came indoors could only sit and murmur over and over: 'What a wonderful night! What a beautiful night!' . . . the stillness was as clear as the moonlight, with sounds for shadows.

Our yard dark. The snow stretching its paws towards the back door.

18, *Sunday.* I came downstairs and saw the snow falling thickly past the window. Occupied myself indoors. Lit the lamp early to write on the kitchen table, and noticed that as soon as I did, the snow had a blue tinge. How it wanders through the dusk! On and on, whiter and more mystic under the branches. My eye rests on this strange distinctness of snow with a lonely sort of joy I cannot explain.

19. The sun shone for the first time in five days . . . shone softly, melting the blue-grey clouds, shone on the big chimney and the Quaker wall, shone into the front room, palely on the shutter.

Last night the rain came, streaming and spouting. The thud, thud! of the waterfall . . . the sound of snow gargling away down the gutters. I heard it going to bed. Got up from horrible dreams and suddenly realized how I hate that dead house—*hate it* and wish they'd pull it down so that I need no longer look at its white windows and ragged bit of awning—faded sottish rag!

Later. M—— walking up to meet me in the old Iceland mackintosh and the blue comforter I knitted him.

Thinking, with a sort of persistent whispering in my brain, I drifted over the dribbling fields. I saw an outward resemblance to my thoughts in the clammy ground, blear hedgerows and foggy trees whose faint colour was the blue of veins. . . . Snow lay along the furrows, clung in knobs to the bank; the earth was rotten with water and stuck to the feet. Only the blackbirds chattered. I heard an axe hacking, and presently saw the boy under an oak. He had hung his jacket on a post and with his thumb was feeling the steel. . . . Dogs chained to kennels barked from gloom, in a smell of straw and mud. The noise of rifles crackled in the mist; cattle bellowed; children and hens squawked and flustered. Once I was made happy. It was when I passed a carpenter's outhouse. It smelled—the sharp smell of wood and glue; the door flung back against the wall showed on its inside where he had tried his colours. As good as many hearty laughs those red and blue and yellow strokes were. The carpenter was planing. Rough water churned along the gutter past his cottage.

20. All of *living* life in the sun! Oh how warm, how reconciled the air! The clouds were bloom on the sunlight though there were black nooks in the sky: the wind and the wonderfully gentle light sifted each other. All was soft, kindly: the full river touching the grass, running with silent power. It's spring. There's a feeling in the wind, a yielding in the cloud, a tenderness in the sun's touch.

How the birds sang—pealing across the fields. One thrush in an ivied branch . . . he was *pounding* with song, trembling like the leaves that hid him.

21. Gloucester a lake city. The barges curved to the yellow water, the blue-black smoke from a tall chimney softly expanding in the clouds. Pant of steam. Then we saw a great old gloomy town house, sooty, and somehow *Roman*. And a row of the most horrible trees I have ever seen, full of terrifying foliage—the leaves dangling yet clotted, with queer red patches, and no light among them.

There is indeed an oddness about M——. He is the dear companion of my faulty nature and physique. If he were ever to be lost to me I should have to think of him as in a natural, earthly, eternity where I could follow him—an immortality of Nature itself—where there would be birds and buds whose kind we knew, dirt, hunger and food, sunlight to lie in, laughter, grumbles, poverty and longing, brown money, celandines, things to hear and things to envy. . . .

Looking at him I think of those fierce Spaniards hurled on the coast of Pembroke hundreds of years ago, one of whose *black* names he has. Oh! how often we have climbed, walked, lazed and lounged together on the hills and in the valleys. That afternoon when we sat in the ditch and the people stared at his gaunt shanks spread over the road, and at me with my bottom and back so comfortable in the dry gutter, trying to make a grass whistle between my thumbs. The sun, the celandines, the greenness of the bank and overhanging trees, how warm, how divinely idle in our untroubled mood!

In Gloucester we went down to the docks, *you* eating chocolate and *me* smoking. I remember the barges and how we passed a hut with the landlady's name on the board, 'Emily Price.'

'I like the name Emily Price.'

'So do I. Emily Price is as good a name as any one could have.'

'Yes. So sturdy. How much money have we got?'

'Threepence—no, tuppence. Tuppence and the tickets.'

And then you pointed out the Roman house: 'I know some one who lived in that grand house.'

We stopped in the square to look at the green grass and the town trees. And in the evening you took me back to the bus.

The night was no more than sky like water, and water like sky, with bars of earth or cloud upon the low lake grey. No stars shone, but the shadowless moonlight breathed a dim motion on heaven and earth. The bus stopped on a bridge and I heard a stream laughing and crying.

22. M—— arrived about eleven just as Pappy was lugging a sack of potatoes into the passage.

It was a soft, warm day with blue among the clouds and a wind that tickled our faces like fur. The sun shone indirectly with the luminousness of vapour . . . like pale golden shadows the fields swelled and sank away among dim hills and clouds of shaded country. Pale washes, wet with light but lineless as air, lay behind the direct strokes of nearer things. As though a hand had drawn the thin curves of budded branches. We went up Penyard which is all hazel woods. Grey and brown . . . the shrivelled blackberry bush like crumpled silver paper. And the dead russet brackens with their tall canes woven into the bones of the trees. We pushed among it all. And then we found a little round gentle spot all vivid moss, with frizzled leaves lying on it, but clear and clean as the floor of a spring. There we stopped. A tractor was shunting round a field below. We heard dogs, voices, cocks crowing, a bell, a trumpet, a sergeant screaming, sheep calling their lambs, birds whistling, trains shunting. It seemed that down there was one version of life, up here another—to live at the roots of trees, to lie at the foot of the sky, to worship low with the seeds.

I drank in the wet smell of sticks—vague, fungoid, which seems of the same reptile quality as the all-coloured grey tree crowds. We laughed from pleasure, not from wit. I never can say or write anything funny, but my humour laughs at its own happiness.

The sunlight swept over the wood like a cloud swelling the sky, and all the trees stood up and swayed. A bird rushed out with a short cry. Before me was a young oak, about my own height. Its top branches were tipped with buds like minarets, beautifully clear and minute: its bark was silver-grey, its lower growth blotted with withered leaves with rolled edges. Under these leaves the buds were clustering close together . . . it seemed almost to be teething. I put out my hand and squeezed a bunch of leaves. They weren't so dry that they crackled, but felt and looked like shrunken chamois leather.

M—— drew my eyes to a strange purple shoot in a brown bush. The hazel buds were showing green twinkles: short grey-green catkins waggled from their twigs. Transparent clouds like the steam of a kettle were rushing over the blue: in the west a rainy and a wood darkness mingled.

We ate our dinner. The man with the tractor stopped for his at the same time, and we heard him start up the engine as we lay back.

Presently some children came up the torrent of a path, roped by their hands. They haunted the trees and rustled the wood for the rest of the afternoon. Once when I was little mother gave me a real Norwegian dress to wear for dressing up, and one small child in black and red and white, flashing every now and again through branches, gave me the feeling of that dress again. The children's voices were more like animals than birds. I heard a yearning, a sharpness or a warning in their cries. The little one sobbed. She had the flaxen hair I never had, but not the little cone cap with its red tassels and coarse white lace.

I saw and longed to gather two oak apples but was too lazy. My body, trained to the accepted ideals of these times, kept sending futile messages. As 'Get up and walk about. Walk over the hill. Do something. Do some knitting.'

I did nothing. M—— did nothing. Gladys grew querulous and I stamped her into sleep.

We talked about this habit of bustling. Work, M—— said regretfully, was a necessity but there could be no such thing as a perpetual necessity. In nature there's no unsatisfiable craving to match civilization's horrible predatory attitude towards 'the next job.' It cannot be virtue to make incessant industry the rhythm and thought of existence. Besides, few modern people ever see the beginning *and* end of their work . . . they are the middle, or the finish or the idea. Work has turned into the abstract *business*—there's no fingering about it, no telling what is happening at either end for both are out of sight. Solids are fast disappearing, and people trade in mathematics.

As it grew colder and the home instinct drew us down from our hill, queer words began to form in my brain: I thought the smooth grained woods were *Hindu Woods*, and the booming breath of life below came to me like a great *land organ*.

So we left the hill, and drank tea and ate toast in a café, and M—— took me back to the Friends' House through the dry dusky alleys. People were drifting: it was the hour when the evening star shines in the grey sky, and the lobster-like motor bicycle creeps out of the rocky passage with polished shell—the hour when footsteps are heard a long way off conjuring empty streets. When he had gone another ghostly night came on. . . .

23. Looked out of my window. A great blue square of moonlight on the road. And along the moonlit garden path the cats came narrowly walking—one, two, three, the last with a horrible mewling voice.

Oh I have done so little, so little! and am no nearer absoluteness. The beautiful star, with its pure, syllable-like rays! Venus, Venus! It shone in the dome of the evening with another faint speck of light beneath it, hollowing the dimness above the houses. To-day the cedar tree seemed dropping soot. . . . Is the moon shining now? The shutters are closed. I must open the door. Yes, but through clouds.

24. A fierce white sunlight beat down between terrific clouds.

The sky was tossed and wild, but yet no wind was felt, no rain fell, only the hills looked dark and maddened.

It was warm, not quite as warm as it has been, but open weather. I went to the Lloyds, but first I slipped through the gate into the orchard where I used to sleep. Oh how often I've sat there with the little 'Eyetalian,' leaning against the bank! But I was alone.

I picked up twigs for Miss —— and a bunch of snowdrops from under my larches. This part of the place was *mine*: my hens scrabbled in these brown needles and here *I* found the purple violets. The snowdrops were springing in that corner by the gate so white that they looked preternatural, so strangely moving!

And under the larches, among tiny quilted leaves, flat to the ground, with their dwarf faces looking up into the pimpled boughs, I saw the first primroses. Oh how I felt! Two of them, only buds this morning from their fresh yellow. Who could explain them? They evoked the same feelings as that still, extended hour of *daylight* reclaimed minute by minute from the winter darkness. They, and the snowdrops, and the buzz of the one lamb are three signs of my beloved, my 'little season.' And that is, in the sky a change, on the earth a sense of the unborn, in me a mood exquisitely balanced between regret for the lovely winter and desire for the change. But I could write forever and never arrive at the subtlety.

I had tea at the Lloyds. They were so kind to me and F—— went with me to the stile. One owl hooted, the bird songs quieted, then stopped. I mustn't forget a tale Mrs. Lloyd told of a woman who suddenly gave up speaking, for good. She would sit in her chair and smile at her family, but never a word. Her son-in-law took her for walks in the meadows, said Mam Lloyd, in one of her gentlest phrases. But she would never go far from the house. She always smiled, then turned back to her place by the fire. When she died, the son-in-law came to Mam and said he should miss her, 'for her never was a bit of trouble, nor never did any harm to anybody all her life.'

25. There goes that teak-faced Mr. B—— in a long black coat, holding his hat in the small of his back.

The people are all soberly walking along the street, all in the one direction—a soldier, a girl, a family, and two men. The road is dry, the children are skipping. In the chestnut trees behind the warehouse a thrush is singing—a thrush is singing as though the world had been prepared for his song. Three notes, then a ravelling.

'Tureen, tureen,' sings he, purling. The sky is so pale that the lightest smoke has body in it.

I have been sawing up the thick trunk of an old apple tree. It took me three days, and now the path is orange with sawdust, with bright yellow and white chips, and amber core.

28. . . . I lifted the curtain. Only the peaceful sound of the rooks flying around and behind the old houses, the stagnancy of stone. The sky was grey, and there were just the top branches of a tree showing above the slates—very thin, like a weed. . . .

It was a strange, vacant moment. A dim light rested on my face. I felt it: but as if so many times filtered through cloud, glass and *flesh*, it was no longer *light*.

I need exorcizing. Now I write this with an old pen I've found, and listen to the old piano that jingles on and on. It must be a music teacher's drudge.

Between half past five and a quarter to seven I walked with Gladys along the river. Writing is explaining; it is nearly always impossible for me to explain. How could I fill anybody else's mind with the evening, the darkening of the air and paling of the ground? . . . more than all the impalpableness which imposes itself gradually between you and what you see—that Nothing which becomes night.

The dusky darkness spread like the network of a great tree. In an elm the thrush was singing. He was so hidden and one with the bushy twigs that I could only see him by his tail which twitched when his song altered. Everything else was motionless except a broken twig which stirred and swung by a strip of bark.

As I went along I made an effort to *climb out* and get into these things—into the mysterious darkening and sealing of the earth, the quietening that is as the loveliest psalm of rest. And at last I did. I stood leaning on a gate. I was behind the sky. I was in the ground. I was in the space between the trees. My meaning grew in the earth and the firmament—I in the Nothing in which all is related.

But when I came out of this I was myself again. I felt cold, eternally solitary. The sun had set in a few dull coaly clouds behind the bank and the sheep were ba-a ba-a-ing. The sound awoke some inexplicable sensation in childhood, and then I felt old. The evening was all dark trees and leaf-lighted ground. Some of the fields were as pale as faded straw. Ah, those reaches by the river! They're so quiet they level me. Their beauty is soothing. There *is* a beauty in a hedgeless path crossing a simple meadow, and big willows rising out of sheep turf.

29. Went shivering over the fields. The lambs' bleating was a plaint of the east wind. Oh bitter wind that starves! Oh miserable, cold, bleakness that makes the earth look forsaken, and the clouds roost on the cheerless hills!

A wretched sunset like a mean fire, at the very back of the orchard. Seen through the bent trunks a dying red—small, small—all the fields small and the sky large, and the bleached blackberry leaves inside out. They had hacked through the young oak. One great limb was down, and it was budding all over with little tan-coloured buds. Half the field was strewn with its last year's leaves. I felt a fury against I don't know what that the quick tree should be destroyed.

Not one bird did I see or hear.

March 2. To-day the wind came rushing out of the bare, blue east, with not so much as a tree or a cloud to ward it off. Ah, it blew bitter! It blew everything loose off the earth. It drove the frizzled oak leaves, so burnt by frost that they were curled like shavings, and it skinned my hands and filled the scoop of my ear with aching roar. But it couldn't move *the light*.

I lay a short while by the river. There was one sun, one tree, one water. The one me lay and looked at the one water where it frilled over a rock. A branch shook near the sun . . . there were still hours of wear in the day. And Johnny Crow lay stark dead on the field, glaring through his dented eye.

3. *Sunday*. I lay on the sun-whitened rock folded in the river, with M——'s hand gripping mine. Again the sky was blue. The swans foamed by us. The water fled away from the sunbeams.

4. A great clear low light shone on the fields this evening, and as the sun sank the world was written across it. The sheep and their lambs galloped up the hill with sky around them, and space in the spaces of their stride. I liked to be there to see them. All that I saw was in my soul with evening quiet about it. How quietly the deep brook ran in the willows! I crept over a plank, from shade to shade. A farm, with cattle and buildings, looked lovely in abiding light. The dipping sun gave to each rut its shadow.

6. After my work went down to the river and picked up sticks. The river had gone down, and rocks under water on Sunday lay low and wet, a deep blackish olive colour.

It was another perfectly still evening with only three sounds—the river, a small bird and a harrow. The sun slipping off the field and going down behind the thorns made me so melancholy and left me so lonely. I was standing by the gate thinking when suddenly I heard the curlew. Its notes were clear, always striking off the last, something in the way that a blacksmith's hammer strikes, before the anvil has done ringing. Clear and high and nearly articulate. At first I thought it was a boy across the river. I asked the fisherman who is often there: 'Is that the curlew?'

'Yes.' He spoke as if we had often talked before: 'Beautiful, isn't it? There's a pair of them nests here somewhere on the bank. He has a nest. You can always hear them in April. He's early.'

The bird appeared in the sky, large and distinct, weeping its notes to earth. It flew in great circles as if searching. Twice it looked, and then seemed to dissolve in the blue transparency. As I went along the bank again it was to be seen slowly circling and crying its wild bereaved cry; I thought it might have been in prison in the sky! As it flew with a sort of *swift slowness* I saw the sunlight that had left the ground, shining on its underwing.

The wing seemed to be bending to an irresistible curve. I never shall forget the ring of the last syllable, the flight which found no flaw of escape wherever it turned, the low trees and high light, and the bird vanishing.

7. It's warm. How weary, weary I feel! My limbs seem crowded into me. The church spire soars out of density . . . long pale pavements with chalk scribbles on the doorsteps. The town when the tide is out. Now the children can play. The birds are singing over the river and I heard the voices of the two boys at L—— Hall, running as Sian and I used to run, using up the last moment of daylight. They play by the same trees and they run back to bed in the twilight, perhaps to the same room . . . the room with a stuffed chaffinch—my cousin Rupert's first shot—in a glass box, and the dark brown linen press. Aunt Nan is coming down the stairs, step by step because of her sore foot. Her hand is on the banisters. I can see her. . . . I heard the curlew again. Its cry is so beautiful that it must have a meaning. To-day there was a wild sort of rapture in the sound, a native loneliness, but it never appeared. L—— Hall, in the black-red sunset, with its high thin elms, stood like a murdered building over the ghastly ground-glimmers.

8. I hurry out when they are sweeping the streets and sweeping the alleys into the streets and swilling the bitten scrubbing brushes in the buckets. I hurry back, when, loosened from their homes, the people drift through the round doors that beat like egg-whisks. The people stick together, to the walls, to the gutters, and the sunlight moves backwards through the solid brick, through willow trees and the river, to the sun itself. I have no time to care: nothing is done for me by myself. My stockings are torn, my legs are ripped and they bleed, my hair is knotty and old and dry. I listen to the heavenly songs . . . to Beethoven's chorus of Creation. Or I sit over paper and ink, knowing that there is still a dark star for grieving. What can I see then but the questionable night?

Later. Restored, I came through the town at midnight walking under the signs which hung motionless over the pavements as if tight in a vice of air. There was the soft swish of a sash window being pushed up and a woman's voice. No traffic. The waterfall was very loud as I came into Brookend. The starlight shone softly bright, not reaching to earth, but illuminating the chasms of the sky with a faint crocus grey. The bent constellations dived westward.

It was a very beautiful, quiet night, warm with the smell of new sap and the sense of young sleep.

I saw the new moon go down in the orchard. Every twig was budding with marvellous detail, breathlessly perfect. The sky was all soft pale grey and pinky-yellow cloud; the meadowland and trees melted my breast and heart! We saw the crows in an inner and outer wheel slowly turning the sky.

13. This is a real country town. A stream flows through it, and in the early mornings one hears jays and woodpeckers.

Oh I am very tired! I want to lie down in the dark room, with one light shining intact and very far away and the remainder of gentle footfalls going past. My soul is haunted by something I haven't written, haven't done, haven't remembered. It's dim as a dream of grass.

18. I sit here with my pen in my hand and there is no beginning and no end, but only ancient patience and long waiting. . . . I walked round the fields. The twilight came by many ways— by cloud, by wind and by moon rays. It darkened quickly. The sparrows' twittering *told me about myself* in small language apt to the subject. They sounded as many consciences together. The gull-grey river was high and furled. From my feet it flowed into the town.

I read somewhere lately some Tennyson, 'the long grey fields at night'—and recognized a reflection 'of that inner physical existence and affinity, of which I am exquisitely conscious, but cannot breathe out. Such a person as myself who cannot speak of these mysteries even to himself, knows in some wonderful way, the shapeless, soundless drift of thought.

I live by intervals of peace, where nothing is spoken but all is comprehended. Or would be if I weren't recalled. One is

THE WINTER JOURNAL

always being summoned. And people want answering. Unless one is in a state of perpetual reciprocity they imagine one to be either mad or angry. One looks *out* suddenly, and sees that, startled, they are waiting for a normal explanation of one's spiritual absence.

Oh I cry when the interruptions become too frequent for endurance, is the earth made to bear such a weight? Can it stand such living on and in and through? Let it rest. Let's all rest. Let's all fall down in the houses, by the roads, in the shops— let's all give way. Why not? But the streets go on changing gear and day is full of work and footsteps and laughter.

19. A while ago I closed the shutters. The evening star was shining above cloud. The wind had a sad, hungry cry in it. Some evil thing took my soul and flew with it. Only something done would have been firmness under me. Well, nothing *was* done. The wind lifting the cloud showed the white town, the dents in the burnished road. It has been wild and rough and dark —doors banging, rooms gloomy with sudden bursts of sinister light before each storm. I have spent the time peeling old paper off the attic walls—thick damp chunks of it which smelled like mould. The great exposed ribs of timber had the bark on them. Draughts spiralled through knot-holes and whistled under the boards. Crows' nests choked the chimney, twigs and litter stuck through the rusty bars of the grate. I scratched and tore at the walls like an old rat while the crows crooned in the flues and the rain fell shattered on the pavement.

Yesterday I had to go and look at the thorn tree by the stile. I had to go right up to it and touch it. It was extraordinary the way it drew me to itself. I remembered it covered with dark red, blackish berries. Suddenly I wanted to find out what had become of them. They were gone. The misty form in the distance separated itself as I approached into branches, twigs and tiny burst buds each with a white split in the husk. The tree teemed with them, but at a few paces distance it still looked the same gaunt black-complexioned thing.

20. Listened to the music. It was full of fearful shadows, the

55

voices of shadows and sudden cruelty. I got up and walked away. It was oh so lovely a night! When I looked out of the window the half moon was shining in the blue sky and the stars were faint and few over the roofs. I saw the street all pitted and wet, the empty pavement. And I longed to be out on the hills hearing the rustle of the sheep. But I went to bed and read of Leviathan, and must have dropped asleep with the book in my hand, for it was open on my breast when I woke. But oh what mountains I passed through before that! I knew that I had passed them through chains of valleys, themselves mountains, and then I was standing in a pleasant field. The light was the queer day of dreams which has no source and is like strong twilight in flat country. The May trees were flowering, a flock of sheep were feeding. Suddenly as I looked beyond the curdled white blossom a gigantic looming figure appeared in the sky, between two clouds, in a lake of fume. The little trees gleamed pearly against it. Sound had fled and even Fear had no cry—the heart stood to meet its enemy. The sheep, now indistinct, were closing their gaps; the sky tightened around us. Slowly the figure lifted from its sides each arm—and stooped. I saw the May trees sicken, the flock stampede, and woke with a frown of torture. The shadow of cockcrow was leaning into the room. My hands were hot fists; straightaway Isaiah's words came into my mind: 'the grass withereth, the flower fadeth.'

22. Night. But very early. Earlier than I have ever known it. Before everything. In the dusk I could still see my ghostly grey hand luminous with plaster dust, stirring the rubbish.

I know that there is in me a growing sympathy. Between the ground I walk on and the centre of my breast, there is love. I can't describe it. I'm not a naturalist or a scholar in leaves and birds, but something is there which makes me stand quite still and look. I do feel a rooted certainty then. The beautiful sky to-day with its streams of gold and grey, its dashes of much blue! And the budding wind, and the hedges alive! A month ago they looked as little like life as a backdoor broom. And oh! the sheep on the mountain the other day, how dear to me!

THE NINTH MONTH IS THE FIRST

SPROUTING from the log I was sawing to-day was a little orange fungus shaped just like a human ear. I touched it and it was fleshy-cold. From it, and a crack in the wood came a clammy cellar-like smell. Later in the day, towards evening, my dog and I were running down to the willow bottom . . .

Somebody had been there and lopped the trees. The great old horizontal boughs were still left looping the stream, but the slender red switches lay scattered on the ground among the rotten stumps, caging the marshy grasses.

The same smell which had emanated from the fungus and the wood crack, was in the mist, in the bark, in the water. The mist was like a mildew in the air, fermenting, rank, and yet the smell was not of it, but carried and wafted by it from the leaves and the wet bark and the layers of soft decay in the earth itself. Powerful, fecund, it almost seemed as if the breath would be drawn out of your nostrils and made to grow into form and shape.

Down by the stream where the moss and grass ends and the sharp green of the marsh-blades pierces water and tussock, down there under the willows and alders where the fallen leaves lay thickest and wettest, seed life in its teeming billions, burst hidden into the world. Rustling over the leaves with my hand I found little blackish-brown balls, cracked and showing the pearl within. From the split in the skin a long white feeler ending in two blanched embryo leaves, smaller than a fly's wings, crept out over the ground, having no roots in the earth, but living from the seed.

On the steep dry bank under the yellow hazel leaves were broken nutshells, celandines, and black-green ivy. Feeling with my hand, passing it gently over and along the tree roots, I saw that at the foot of the spindle tree a mouse or bird had mounded up little heaps of the berries where the leaves disguised but did not bury them. These, too, were opened, revealing the vivid seed within the lovely petal-like sheath.

Sifting the golden hazel and dark copper willow leaves, I saw and touched the earth. Soft and red, taking the impression of the finger-tip like dull wax, it lay hidden under the life which had died against it. It smelt of fermenting juices. Touching it I felt its clinging, living coldness mounting the veins of my arm, drawing me down into it. Under the dead bracken, the ivy, the celandine, and fox-glove it lay, lapping minute birth, minute decay. I saw the berry's kernel, the emptied broken nutshell, the flex of the shrivelled grass root like a nerve exposed. The sting of the dying nettle, the prickle of an autumn weed, the sprout of a seed, each told me something. Under the leaves, under the branches, rotting, germinating, preparing, a hundred years were there to come. The ground was teeming, yielding everywhere for life to issue out. Ferns and celandine (with two wan blossoms), violets, foxgloves, primroses and lords and ladies, wild strawberry and wood sorrel, all were waiting with ages before them, creeping and decaying, making ready, dying limp against the bank, yet shooting forth and beginning again. The earliest, eagerest spring watcher begins to tingle no sooner than the end of January when he bends to the snowdrop and the aconite; yet here in this November budding thicket, dark and leafless, all the year is ready.

The grass is whitened at the tips, but vivid green moss grows round the bases of the trees. The alders bend over the path and the stream—the beautiful alders filled with little close-smooth mauve and silvery catkins, like shreds of light hanging in the mist. All their twigs curve upward at the tips. At a distance there is something solemn and deadening in the alder's look, though lovely in its cloudy tone, indescribable by any clear term—but close to, the almost movement-growth and this happy upward tendency makes it the most exquisite of trees.

As I bend to the ground to brush away the leaves, the trees seem to cower, and their dark branches sink, and their torsos grow squat, but as I rise they soar up from me, and the small grey birds seem higher and more shrill. I hear the thrush singing in the mist: 'Turee, turee,' sings he in loud and perfect song from the orchard above. 'Chink, chink, chink,' goes the blackbird along the hedge. It is evening and the trees are dim with the thickening of dusk. All the colour is in them, in the bark and the yellow-green willow boughs, the crocus-hued catkins, and the golden and green moss. The sky is mist, the field is pale; the white axe scars show up more clearly on the clubbed willows, the arch made by the flying chips is almost visible from their distances upon the ground. It is so soft walking the feet make no sound upon the turf. There is no sound but the brook and the thrush—and then suddenly a pigeon bursting out of cover is like a bough falling, and an old horse stretching his neck and shaking his shoulders from an invisible collar, goes shambling down to drink.

It seems not darker, but *whiter* and yet one can see less. All the birds are enlarged and slowed in their flight by the mist. A flock of sheep running down the field makes a noise with their hooves like streams pouring. I can hear their sides pressed and rubbing together, and then as if by the beat of a drum, they stop, a panting, greyish mass, craning over the hill . . .

At home the lilac bush is in bud, and here the staff of the honeysuckle sprouts beads of green. Although the nettles are going down into the earth, and the hardiest weeds are yellowing and the air is empty of insect flight, it is the month of germination, the first era of growth. I can taste germination on my tongue and at the back of my throat. The fog and the rain are fertile. The seed-ball expands and the earth around will contract with frost until the tenderer matter bursts and the finite plant is born in the infinite earth. Stalks, leaves and husks rot and peel away from the living germ that it may be born new to itself. Not only in thrusting forth, but in decaying and folding back are the processes begun. The ground under my feet is teeming with shoots and suckers and seeds, with all kinds of nurslings shut off from too much light.

At this season all growing things are at their most perishable stage, still feeding from the husk as it shrivels, still blindly attached, still too weak and tender to be fed direct from the adult earth. The bud must drink from the parent tree, and the child tree be fed from the fruit. In the earth is the food of maturity, of strength, the sap of oaks, the juice of full power and beauty. It must be filtered, strained and diluted through nursing channels before the seedling may drink it. Think of it! Every tree, grass and plant you see, is a river, a green spring flowing upward. Every grass lifts some hidden essence from immovable darkness into the light and wind!

And some of these things, the smallest of them, the stream and the trees told me I should see. I should touch their flowers and feel their glistening colours. The youngest, swiftest, and most forward of them perhaps . . . soon. The thought entered the air, and made everything more distinct and lovely, more bright and clear, real and precious.

The slowest of them, those of mineral tardiness, the iron-old tree, and the grey hundred-haired brake, I shall never see but in unrecognizably young versions of their forms. But for to-day, and for next year, it is enough just to wander up and down the stream, just to see the catkins hanging down, to hear the thrush, and touch the small buds.

BEFORE THE SNOW

THE NOW OF IT

THE pile of books in the window has gone down by one since I reached for my own thick volume of notes to copy out this writing. But it won't be copied . . . the sense of the marvellous is too strong, the marvellous complete and vivid moment in which I am breathing and seeing, lights even these once spontaneous but now dead lines with fresh detail, and deeper thought than they possess in themselves. The task will be a long one. As the tree swells over its shadow, as the new hill covers the recent land of delight, the present overlays the past, insisting by every sound, movement, every tone and shape, that the senses shall dwell in it *alone*. If you want to write with absolute truth and with the ease of a natural function, write from your eyes and ears, and your touch, in the very now where you find yourself alive wherever it may be. Carry your paper and book with you and conceal yourself in the fields. Watch and *be* in what you see or in what you feel in your brain. There is no substitute even in divine imagination for the touch of the moment, the touch of the daylight on the dream. In sleep we are given light to see our creation and a moment to last: and it is best so, in waking, to let the sky and the earth, the trees and the water, into our own thoughts and the thoughts of our inner people who are, after all, but other selves clothed in separateness and walking apart.

Even so there is a fading, a merging, a loss of *something* which no pondering and no effort can bring back. We are bound to return some time and to begin 'copying out.' Once that starts . . . well to be within walls, even close under an open window where you can see rooks flying and calling under the clouds, is to be in comparative darkness. However light the room in which you work, it has few living shadows and little space compared to the field in which you saw so clearly. You may picture it with all the vividness in your power, but *where* is the grass you actually saw, the real grass with separate blades, with moss in it and roots and the light roughing it? It is not in you. Recollect the trees as you may, something is gone out of the vision. You cannot call up the colour of the bark, the seaminess, the firm flakes. A joy which rested on the ground and filled the sky, is not to be described. The brain wearies toiling with language, and the captive sight follows the bird's flight over the elm tops with a deep unconscious longing to return to the 'now' which seemed so unbreakable when you rested in the field only a short while ago. 'How was this and how was that,' you find yourself asking. Almost a *sense* seems to elude you, and you read with despair what you have been trying to write of that close infinite Past. It is only words, only yourself. Everything in the room around you belongs to your life and can tell you nothing fresh, whereas the lost element in your sum of life was an indefinable presence, or spirit *outside* yourself surging in the passing air as it lifted the grey hazel branches and turned over the dead leaves on the meadow.

All good, true and *loving* earth writing must be done first out of doors, either spontaneously in the brain or roughly and livingly with the hand, then afterwards, as swiftly translated to permanent wording as may be. Translated to permanence—ah, is there, *can* there be permanence? *with* life! The only chance is swiftness and intensity of feeling. Or else, as fallen snow obliterates all movement and knowledge, time *lightens* the impression and the precious secrets discovered are hidden moment by moment in the day of ever fresh discoveries.

I believe that the most lucent form of writing one's thoughts in earth (as distinct from the thoughts in the brain) is in Notes or daily journals. It is most difficult and most painful to rely on memory, which having its own tricks of colour and its own tastes, is always ready to substitute and to reform. The body has no past. The limbs and the skin feel minute by minute—the physical is always the now. If you want to keep your sensations, which are bodily thoughts, as exquisite and subtle as they are powerful, then be swift or they will shrivel like insects' wings and some beauty and some knowledge will have gone out of the world.

I am writing this at a table which I have pushed under the window. It snowed in the night, and the window faces the winter east. I saw the sun rise behind the oak trees. The sky then was clear red and hollow green. The rooks flew high, by threes at a time, fast and silently. The oaks were of a strange green darkness, the limes, farther south, pure naked black.

The deep chill in the air is like a smell—the smell of the snow. It breathes into the room, it can be smelt all over the house. It is like a smell and like a light not shining but penetrating every corner with calm intensity. The silence is like a roar! When sound comes it seems to pass by the ear, close against the drum, with a palpable tremor in the brain. Close, close and loud is the whirr of the sparrows' wings as they drop on the path. And large and sharp is the blackbird's jet wing in the infinitesimal minute before he settles on the wall. The crumbs I have thrown out look large and dirty. Everything that is not snow looks so— bricks, stones, footprints, grey as thick glass. . . .

There is no sky, only a yellowish density which emphasizes the ground glare. And no light but that which the flat field throws upward. In the sun is no light. No light but a presence just visible and without influence. A lantern burning in a whitewashed outhouse long after daylight has just such a presence. It is not dimness but powerlessness. White-sided earth and thick seamless vapour has made a daylight lantern of the sun.

I look, not at the sun but at the sun's place just above the fir tree. I look at the arctic daylight of the fields and hills. The stream must be a black crack in the snow with corners and sharp bends, and the sound of water running drop by drop from twig to stone, drop by drop under the white rafters. So sensitive has the silence made my ears that it seems to me that I can hear it trickling by even from here. Its voice is like the broken notes of the birds who cry out plaintively now and again as they perch on the posts and clothes-line, from there dropping to the path and gradually getting nearer to the doorstep by starts and broken flights. Each downward swoop from the hedge is a repetition of the last 'whirr-whirr.' Then the silent and suddenly distinct little shape begins hopping backwards and forwards and sideways, all the time with its eye turned up to the window and its beak at an angle between fear and entreaty, its tail tracing half circles above the level of its head as the bird on its spring-like feet flicks itself lightly round in the snow. Some of the dead leaf shapes (a few sprays of black bramble for instance), and this lively hungry dancing of sparrows and tits against the vast snow, is like a dark scintillation. Every movement strikes as intensely, or separately, on the eye as does the slightest noise on the ear.

The blackbirds and thrushes hop heavily away, slow, unwilling to leave the neighbourhood of human food. So out goes more cold potato and a saucer of water which freezes into wrinkles. Through the glass I watch them feeding. But to me it is as if the yellow in the blue-tit's breast is tinged with the murk of the sky.

Again comes the snow driving through the hedge with a hissing like frozen reeds clashing. The fields are raised above the molehills, the hedges are thorny brown, poles supporting their heavy eaves. When the storm is over every track and path is hidden. The earth stretches away up and down hill between and beyond the openings, white, monotonous, unrecognizable, with no relief of tone but faint ghostly grey circles under the great trees. Often I have imagined that I should know all the land about me if it were uncovered to the depth of six feet. I should know it by the roots and the directions of the rocks, by the falls of the flayed valleys. But looking at it changed by the snow I do not feel so sure. The evenness, the glitterless blank does away with direction. Direction is a course and sense. Thought in and love of a place shed a transparency on the ground—and yet how little we are aware of what *is*, even on the surface.

This morning brought many realizations of secret movements and wild life lived at different moments from our own. In the night and the early morning the birds and the beasts wandered over the untouched fields leaving a record of their unremarked existence for the daylight to reveal. It caused one a mystic kind of amazement at the heart just to see the home cat's trail winding round the garden plots and up the outhouse roofs. And M——— came back with tidings of where rabbits had rested and over which slopes the fox had slanted to his earth. Some saw badger tracks, or said they did. But some will always see badgers for other people's foxes and hares for their rabbits. But that which startled and touched most suddenly the nerve of perception were the bird tracks. I never remember *realizing* flight as I did when out in a field some distance from the hedge I looked down and saw the treble markings I had followed cease—just stop without flurry or fading as if some natural thought had lifted the bird out of the world. The lonely snow and there being nothing after those last prints. I despair of describing the effect, but it lay in that which was missing, rather than in that which was there. The human record was complete: men never seemed more numerous or more solid, leaving as they did one neighbourhood for another and all linked by plodded tracks. Their very purposes were as naked as the snow. Between those narrow scutted ruts each made by the thrusting forth of a heavy foot not lifted but pushed forward over the earth, lay no space for guessing. The tracks were pickets, tying the maker to the peg and the peg was home. Just as far as his work lay from his fireside, the rope that is in the heel of every man, uncoiled over the fields without giving one unnecessary loop to freedom.

Later. M——— said he thought he saw a goldfinch in the snowy garden, flying along the wall . . . the tom-tits were whirling their wings in the thorn trees, the hazel catkins hung out in the pale sunlight which was like a shade on the chalk-white slope. It was thawing, a loose wind blew as if from nowhere like a coat slipping off the shoulders. The stubble points appeared, the flattened molehills, and at last a soft and brilliant land, dark with wet colours. To stand outside in the warmth, to breathe and look was to feel the body made of thought. . . . At night part of the Plough shone like a bridge tossed up into the sky. The moon, at a blunt angle from the flattened hilltop, cast a shadow from the elm which divided the east and west.

BEFORE THE SNOW

SECOND PART

WE have had small snow falling, but the prevalent mood of the weather was frosty. Walking over the trampled bracken under the great oaks and chestnuts I notice how the blackberry bushes have dwindled to the ground. Their leaves have rolled themselves into pale silvery-grey tubes on the outsides of which the veins are raised; they rattle like tin-foil on the stems, and break if you touch them, into pieces or even into dust, so dry, so parched are they by the burning frost. Inside the hedges and bushes and among the low thorn branches, the birds are seen jumping from perch to perch like darkened leaves which flutter but never fall to the ground. They don't sing but utter in few notes the sensation of cold, of emptiness. Only the robin sings . . . his icy song, sharp as sleet, breaks from a blackthorn after I have passed, deriding me, and the weather, the other birds and the musical ringing silence which answers him.

I stop for a moment to look at the colour of the blackthorn. It is a beautiful dark-damson red, polished, every thorn distinct and finished. As I stand some magpies begin to be very active around an oak tree, and the woodpecker flies into the top of an elm. A beautiful sky is unrolling beyond the still branches and twigs. The tits and chaffinches go up and down the twigs against the swift cross movement of the clouds. Far away crows break into many languages, and starlings whistle. When I come home and sit by the fire I don't think but just see the pattern the birds made—just see *things* as they were—the willow leaves lying on the sheep track, on the heavy frost-bleached grass. They are like little yellow fishes glinting. Between the tree roofs and under the boughs it is twilight, and my hand goes groping over the dry leaves and moss, feeling for sticks to put in the sack.

The tips of the grasses are withered and pale. When it is not freezing it is like walking on soft fur. Only the moss is living. The fields are neither white, nor brown, nor grey, but all of these at once. In the sky small single stars begin to shine, brightening the air but spreading no light. They make me think of wild flowers: they don't seem to ask to be looked at. Evening is to Day what winter is to the year . . . only little flowers and little stars bloom in its woody paths. The deeper I look into the pure, round evening star the clearer in me grows the image of the snowdrop, so full of its own fairness, so compact of light!

Evening-dusk! The voices of the children playing under the apple trees, the horses feeding by the brook. Snap, snap, go the sticks into the sack. Then suddenly, after the blackbird's roosting cry, 'Tink, tink, tink,' the silence in the cove of the trees, the sunset, the foam in the sound of the stream rushing round the bend under the alders and willows. Beautiful is the position of the alders, the bending to pour shadow into the clear water, the tenderness in the stoop. Their branches grow in protection over the white ripples. It would hide the pools where the hill water spouts through ferns to the sandy bottom. But the light is gone and the stream seems hidden in its music, and all the tributary sounds—the birds, the children's shouts, the stab of a horse's hoof against a fallen trunk—are silenced.

My sack of kindling is full. I lift it on my shoulder and spring from the ozzy stone across to the other bank. Soon I am at the gate. The touch of the iron chain going back into childhood, coming always as a finish to the fields! Now my hand is pushing the smooth stick into the staple; now there is only the road going up the hill to our path. See and mark the brush-like twigs bunching from the lower girth of the elms. You will remember them as if they were an era. Look at them so slender and brushy, growing straight out horizontally from the huge trunk. Do you think that you will be able to carry them home in your mind? Do you think that when you sit down to-night with your paper and pencil you will be able to write of this moment of feeling and all that is contained in its circle?—the furled colours, the purple and red and wine wound within the bramble-leaf tube, the ploughed fields, the mossy grass, the willow leaves, the stars and the trees bursting like fountains from the hill bends, their stems concealed in the earth curves, their branches shooting upward from the grass? Watch the hedgerow, the bank with its dusky gaps, the lane, watch how a breeze is moving all the stillness like a wave towards you. Do you think that movement will come back when the paper is spread out for you to write? No: it never will. All this and you are in the 'now.' Move, and you are in another, with the creaking of a window, and breathing and a fire burning. Far as you will be from this moment, too far even to remember the details of its existence, you will be farther from its meaning.

On top of the bank the sheep are standing and lying out in the field, on the edge of the bright dying sky. Their fleeces are haloed against the opposite swell of ploughed land. They aren't feeding but resting on the grass, or looking down over the hedge at me standing below the bank. I see their hatchet-like heads and necks thrust into a gathering of light. Between their legs and under their bellies is the gloom of the valley. Noiselessly those which are lying down lift and turn their heads to search for my presence. They listen . . . I listen. I hear the stream and a faint movement in the dead leaves under the bank. Nothing else. No voices and no tread near or far. Even the ivy round the trunks of the trees is not fluttering but hangs as still as I have seen it on a summer morning when the sun strikes straight upon the leaves. The sky seems waiting for the moonlight.

.   .   .   .

In the evening I put down my thimble and the shirt I was patching and went to the door. The stars seemed to push under the eaves and to shine against the stone wall. The moon had risen half an hour before and now she was free and strong in flight. White as new silver she had neither clouds nor rainbow circle but shed the reflection of her own stark body over the field and the wall and the trees. Hers is not living fertile light, like the sun's, but an embalmment on rocks. She flew fast over the lime trees, casting elbows of shadow far over the clover. Was the power in the air, in the moon, or in the sky? A huge and silent scheme of wheels seemed inter-revolving over and through the earth. I stood on the path. Not a breeze wrinkled the air. The buds on the lilac bush were pointed and motionless. . . .

Birdless was the garden when in the moonlit dawn I went to fetch coal. All night through the glass-clear atmosphere, frost particles had fallen and gathered on the windows, on the wire line—frost dust furred bark and branch, thorn and window. The log across the sawing horse was white, the dim rows of winter greens gleamed greyish-dusk, the stones were frozen to the ground. Around the moon the sky was the same blue as the flame of the lamp indoors.

From the door to the coal-heap, from the wood pile to the fire, I journey over and over, noticing how the sky over the wall is paler each time I lift my eyes. The moon shines on, turning from silver white to a deep ripe apricot, setting not in the horizon but in the daylight. When I go down the garden she is going and when I turn round she is gone, and the birds are beginning to fly. Oh if I had the language I would write poems to the birds' waking, poems of their first flight into the day. Listening, seeing, *living* this first hour, each moment seems dipped up from a clear profundity of leisure, each breath is a sweet and tingling swallow of eternity to them and to me. They flutter, they arch in the air, they try their wings and their voices. One by one sparrows, tits and chaffinches awake, sound their notes and leap through the air. Starlings in the hollies add their noise, and at last, as the east quickens and kindles, the crows swoop forth from the brown oak branches, through the stream and river valleys, flying low and crowdedly in and out of the hills cawing, shrieking, squeaking and yet all in concord with one sound in all the many, as waves, and bees, and all multitudinous things. High overhead or low in the distance I love to hear the crows, so rich, so warm is their throaty calling, like a sun-curdling cloud of sound behind the fields, like a cityful of people in the tree tops all happy together, all pleased to get up and begin the day. . . .

It is light—and everybody is moving to work and I am standing in the garden patch with a bucketful of coal. The sheep, and the children running to school, that man plodding over the field with his tools on his back, all spout silver breath. Our lungs fill without effort, our voices call as if of themselves. Even going to work has something wonderful about it, even going down the garden path is a long enough journey to forget one's purpose. Isn't a purpose waiting for you in the air, an excuse in the sight of the sun? The eye and brain are filled with life, visible and invisible, wonderful and strange. The sun dawns with meaning into the world. He sends great red beams down to the blue-grey fields and the backs of the birds glow as they span the hedges in flight. The black legs and faces of the sheep are stressed in the pale misty ground-air, till it seems one can see the skeleton of the flock within its rounded, hoary body. Pressed against the gate they are waiting for Bob to drive them down to the valley meadows to be fed.

Later. Birds float and call in the wintry spaces—rooks in careless pairs uttering their slow wide-apart cries, sparrows rustling among the fallen cabbage leaves and frost-furred poultry wire. As I go along the rows of greens ripping off sprouts for dinner a great flying wedge of sparrows dives like a missile into the far hedge and after shrewdly estimating the distance between us, scatters in quick movement about the garden.

There have been days this autumn and winter when the *sky* has been birds—endless spreading clouds of them, crows, pigeons, gulls, starlings, stretching darkness over the bend of a hill as they rise with a roar from feeding. They hear your footfall, and it is exactly as when a wind blows on a bonfire whirling burnt straw, black paper and wood ash up into the sky, to sink again farther off in slowly spinning columns.

Lately, on my journeys to get sticks, I have been crossing the field of barley stubble. I have trodden on the site of the lark's nest, where he rose from his mate as she sat close among the stalks. Surely, for me, the memory of his song has made a natural shrine out of unmarked earth and dry and withered weeds. Cold winds and frost have parched the stubble which, green and supple, threw its growing shadows over her back: the sheep have gnawed the clover down to the hard, red ground, have lain and trodden it into one huge solid brick of red plaster, bound with dead and living fibres in which are stuck the dead-glinting hollow bristles of the decapitated barley. The wind swishes, the winter sun hovers low over the place: the moles have tunnelled it and thrown up rough red cones of frozen crumbling soil; the oaks in the next field are bare of their brittle brown leaves. Yet he, the lark, that small spirit of a bird, in body like a pebble flung from a boy's catapult, in voice incarnate music, he still appears there to me, in fact and in imagination, in being, and in memory of song. Every note comes back, as if given out of a more distant ether, music of the rain and sun—rain which is now the sea, sun which is in the trees and the blood of men!

Stop for a moment I must, whether my sack is empty or heavy on my back, just as I would if he were in danger. My feet are on the very spot where he used to rise and begin the endless unwinding of his thread of notes. In the trackless cold I may stand an hour and leave no footprint, and the air has taken to itself the atoms of his home and left no regret in him. Yet something keeps him in the neighbourhood, some echo of his last year's life he feels, for I see him nearly every time I pass, flying nearby three or four feet above the field as if attached by lease or love to something in the place. He is not so much flying, as *on the wing*, following, as it were, a tangle of air paths, but never soaring and seldom uttering a note. Once I saw him begin to mount, letting fall as he did a few drops of song, but he soon alighted and flew brokenly around as usual. Often two of them are together. Yet I cannot tell, neither have I been able to find out from books or people, whether the lark is a bird which mates for life. The books describe his feet, his colour, his eggs, his habit, but not his spirit of song; his nest they tell of but never his love. As for the humans they cannot answer for they don't seem either to know or to care about knowing. Now I can't be content without this small fact: to me it is something missing out of my universe; and by some means or other I will find out whether this is my lark and his wife and whether bound by lifelong bond they will live out their contract with the earth and sun in this same field.

The flocks of birds are over, the moles under the earth. Under the close colourless grass, under the corn stubble, under the garden patches, those blind snouts have bored miles of slightly arched tunnelling, have pushed up whole towns and settlements of dark-red kraals. There is a fresh colony on the way down to the valley and another just clear of the trees' shadows by the stream. They are frozen hard as boulders: the frost on the dark-red earth shows glassily, like snail tracks on a path, and in the cracks and crumblings, as in the whorls of the cow pats, glimmers a grey secretion of hoar dust.

Hard, hard, baked in the furnace of the burning cold, burnt, parched in the flame of frost, is the ground round the roots. The surface of the earth crackles like a cured skin, the bark is rigid round the tree, the arterial waters have shrunk to veins. The sky is one great curved jewel, now crystal blue, now opal white, charged with surging whirling particles, seen in the air against the Infinite, in millions upon millions. Are they *seen* or a part of sight? Is this light-dust eternal dancing in the deeps of the sky or in the deeps of my own eye? I cannot tell, but when I stare upwards into the blue zenith the sparkling air divides itself into unspeakably bright atoms ever moving, ever descending upon the eyeball like sparks of lightning, like unformed colour, like the sun inchoate in the void.

All these days the horizons lay hidden in the substance of the earth and sky, cloaked in an emanation which is of neither and of both; a tone, a shade, a ring of softest mist in which the uprightness of the trees and the corners of the hills are half seen and half submerged. The edge of the earth seems to belong to the sky, and the low cloud circle to the ground. The sun nestles in the hills and close in them his rays seem to meet and mix with a final solidity. The breath of earth mingling with his pure winter rays turns them to colours like odours, soft and dense.

He hovers there morning and evening, resting near the hills, but through the zenith he flies with visible speed, rushing hurtling over the trees and roofs, making the central hills seem small and noon-like and this field and cottage the centre of his dial.

For a short while the true day sunlight rests on the dry grey grass, and the marrowless stalks of oats, glinting on the silvery-brown thistles where they stand up in the pastures dry and dead, shrivelled and rustling. Odourless, dry and rigid as if baked under parching rays, the earth masks itself with yesterday . . . with a pause under which its channels run with pressing, fluent life. The air is like wings to the body, a breath seems to raise it; the lifted foot is light and leaves no stain or bruise upon the ground where it has trodden.

From the lark's shrine in winter I can see the curved lines of trees, the indigo elm trunks clumped about the land, the clouds glimmering like the edges of the moon. The grey-blue shadowy hills lie over the fainter violet shadow of the horizon. And the horizon is not the end of earth but the indefinite edge of the atmosphere, where it clears behind a familiar outline of ploughed hill and thorn hedge. Shade crosses shade, deepening, lightening; but the radiance which sparkles from the swift white sun strangely, subtly is connected with darkness. Looking far far across the land into the end of sight I see this brilliance between me and the fields, between the branches, dropping like a curtain of atoms between my eyes and the sun, and I know it for what it is—very winter, and the darkness in the crystal.

Over my shoulder as I sit on an elm root by the bank, touching me on the eyelids, the sun comes down into the world. I turn my head and I see its fire-white sphere low in the heavens between two earth clefts, as if it would roll quietly down the meadow to the water side. The sudden sense of nearness is like a message in a touch. The sky above me is infinite, a broad, bright river stretching from haze to haze, clear and bottomless in its light. But the sun has come near to me and is part of my world. The water thrills, the sear grass shines, the blooming plough lands refract the beams as pure darkness to pure light.

It is in moments like these that the January dandelions flower, and the mind is filled with the exquisite rarity of winter's images, the lovely detail of its space, the perfect sounds of peace and work.

I am resting and over the dark mirror of my mind, cleared by the silence, passes a bird's bare flight, a fox's gliding gait. I have a thought which tells me in no language which I can reproduce, how the hearing selects sounds matched to the body's occupation. Rest and you hear peace breathing, work and you hear the world stirring around you. It is as though the ears choose rhythms and harmonies to the time. When I am digging I hear others working in the gardens and fields and hedges. I hear the thud of the axe, the blow of the stake beetle driving the post deep into the bank; across the fields come thought, as well as sound harmonies.

Drawing water from the butt as the ice sags and cracks and the water flows unwillingly into the bucket, I hear in my mind the stream singing, I see the bubbles dancing by the sandy submerged ridges like little domes of glass riding on the undulations of the brown and golden water, swept away with the twigs, the fallen catkins, the minute scales of lichen, towards the gloomy arch of the bridge.

But in restful moments when the work is done or pausing, as I stand breathing out my thick breath into the air, sounds of stillness come to my ears, bringing an indescribable peace, illuminated and still, to all the worlds of my brain. The moments expand. All the painful microscopic plans which riddle away the glorious day, shrink and die, less than the least of the most minute bacteria which thrive upon the flesh. Then as sound by sound, the natural world becomes real, a transparency is substituted for impenetrable matter and I can see as if I were present in some less hostile form than human, the row of silent hives in my neighbour's garden, the ceaseless careless flights of the birds from eaves to branches, when no one is there to make them shy and wary. More; without mental effort I can become as the wind, as the very light, entering the barn doors and the crannies in the stones, learning how things are in the hibernating insect world, discovering the bats behind the cartshed wall, the wild bees and wasps in the banks, the flies, the buried and suspended chrysalises hanging in the corners of workshop windows where dust and frost have made the panes as dull as cowhorn.

To and fro over the expanse of fields and trees and streams, led from sound to sound—led by sound up into the air and down below the level of the earth to where the snakes are sleeping with their eyes glazed, consciousness roams while one's body rests in an unconsciousness even of existence. All that one sees and hears exists and is beautiful, mysterious, full of meaning. Far away with the bees in their cells, yet one hears and loves the elms uttering the wind, the nearby blue-tits hopping round and round, blurs of green and yellow and blue mixed by movement like the colours on a top. All is simultaneous. Therein lives the uncommunicable wonder, the difficulty of writing. The hues, the sun, the livingness in the eye, that which is in the mind and that which lives around and is seen, they are all simultaneous. Consciousness has many layers, profundity on profundity. For this one and separate miracles, the universe, the now, substitute words which must be added one after another, and the vision finishes as a list.

If I might by a spiritual process unknown, undeliberated, mark the paper with one minute's eternal variety so that all who looked might understand what was there—then I could understand what *makes* such people as myself try, by any means they can, to reproduce and retain some record tangible, detached from themselves, of what they see and love in the earth. But I cannot—I cannot. The air and the light will not get into the paper. The hills are forgotten and the floor and the ceiling crush my thoughts between them. Beginning to write before I knew all the shapes of the letters—long before I cared to *read*—I have found myself where I was when I first started with fairy stories, to utter what in my human translation meant the feeling in inhuman life.

It is my belief that fairy tales are Nature writing; that the grass-tall people *are* the grass, or at least an ideal race created by children and nature spirits such as Hans Andersen's, who so love and adore grass and leaves, trees and ferns, moor and mountain

75

and solitude from man, that they can only exist by touching these things and breathing their breath. Nearer to the spirit of the now than any poet or naturalist who ever sighed over paper, are children's own fairy tales about the lives and feelings of beasts, the speech between clouds and plants and the conscious spirit in the elements.

That there *is* a consciousness in all living things I am certain. But as I grew up and began to live, as most of us have to, longer drearier hours indoors, I lost not the sense of it, but the hope that it might be intercepted and partly understood. Wherever I go I must carry with me speech in my mouth and brain which is as uncomprehensible to the other kinds of being as the sparrows' jangling is to me.

Not only that: but I must be inadequate in my own language, tedious, unilluminating in my attempts at communication with my own sort. I must use words which I loathe when I would go beyond words, write beyond print, show more of moments, days, of life, than paper can take. How long, how long I am trying—I have had to brush away the dust from this page, yet all the time since I last touched it some of my thoughts have been resting on it, pressing on its surface, as my thoughts press into my brain. At last this white oblong half covered with words, pushed into a shut book and apparently disregarded, has become almost an inner part of me.

Sickened by jargon I left it, sickened as one might be by one's own diseased limb. 'Thought harmony!' Those words which should mean so much *mean nothing*—they are as near the spirit of the kind of harmony I know as the jay's screech is to the thrush's wonderful cooling song. That is because I am not apt at matching words to thoughts. I am short of words, short of names for beauty and joy, rest and energy. I could not go out on a May day and call all the things in my garden by name, not the weeds nor the flowers, to say nothing of the flies and little coloured bettles which crawl out on the twigs over the path. And I cannot tell of them without our having a common symbol between us, and so I must learn more, twisting away from them, to a closer understanding with people risking the infinite loss of the direct and wordless touch of the earth.

As a child, as all children, I put myself into what I saw. It was instinctive in me to humanize trees, stones, bushes. Instinctive and easy. But within my play, behind and within, and under me, I realized, at times, another stronger existence—and occasionally as I grew older I *felt* towards it. Rarely, but consciously, then more often, and still more vividly. Yet more often I played on the surface, idealizing the chance way stones lay about and plants grew. Avidly the child spirit reached out, grasping the beauty and interest of the world, touching, absorbing its places and crying to itself of everything 'Mine, mine.'

No.

Twenty years. More than twenty years with only as many separate enlightened moments, to learn that the moments were of the truth and the years of self-seeing. In those moments came the realization that the things I saw limited myself to myself. That I must not try to graft my imagination on to the earth, if I wished to comprehend our differences, and our profound, common soul.

I believe the soul to be universal—an element, one element in all things. All things, even inanimate ones, have a kind of life, most of them a separate one as well as the universal and spiritual meaning, common to all. The detail of earth and sky, the clouds, stars, winds, birds, animals, all the lists we have to make when writing of the one spontaneous 'aroundness' are living in one living element, one comprehension, ourselves too included, as the detail and pattern of a man's brain is included in his unknown spiritual being.

I have thought this, not in words but in breath, standing, running, living, sleeping.

Before I came in to write it the song of a robin brought it into my mind, and the sight of a certain tree across the stubble. It is in the lark's voice; in the seasons, in the separate and long moments which I call the 'now,' whose steady sequence is living consciousness. Sometimes it is clearer and more beautiful, as though there were sunlight in the brain showing the brightness in the threads of thought, illuminating the cells where the

77

ideas are born. And sometimes it is only a dark feeling like instinct, like the feeling of things at night when you cannot see them but *sense* them as forms absorbing space.

But it is always there. . . .

What *makes* me see this or that tree at some moment when I am not thinking? What brings the actual flat stem of the reddish climbing ivy before my inner eye? I can see each leaf, each angle of the spray as it clings to a certain old grey ash post. And I can see the chrysalis hanging in the frosty corner of our kitchen window. It is white and greyish, spotted with black and green like a lichened twig. The forepart is pointed with a single horn-like projection.

As I am writing this men are busy grubbing up old fruit trees and laying hedges. A high load of tangled brushwood for kindling has been piled by our wall. In this false 'bush' a robin has come to live and every morning when I am washing up he sings. His voice takes me out into the open light, makes me long for the fields. To-day M—— told me about the stake beetle. It is a rough club made of withy and is used to drive in the sharpened stakes of holly and ash and hazel. In and out of these the browst or brushwood is woven in with the living growth to make a sound wind-proof hedge.

As they hack with axe and hook the men pull the boughs away and pile them behind them like another hedge. I hear the blows, the booming, the thudding and the dragging. The chips arch through the air, white against the cloud, and drop onto the stubble.

I love the clean substance of the ash, its smooth olive bark, its golden rind to which the white wood flesh clings. The alder will only smoulder. Its body is water. You cannot burn the brook. But willow burns with earnestness, sending out dreams of scent on the smoke. The spindle tree, the tree the devil hung his mother on—that is gone too. And a huge ash, carved into blocks for gateposts, stares on the ground, a white work-place which left at evening still seems to ring with the chopper. Thorn, ash, elder, hazel, holly, all have come down and instead of groves there are upward and downward dipping new hedges, strangely artificial. In the evening I walk along and see more of the hills, and a new vision of the land. Looking at the position of the chips, at the way things lie, the workers seem vividly present. Thus they swung the axe—thud thud, over the fields echo the blows' crackle, and tearing sounds through the lanes. The men's presence is a fresh and powerful impression; the day is closer than the dusk.

After tea their children go to collect for the fire, with sacks, trolleys and baskets. Two little boys and a girl are crackling among the sticks. Sliding in and out of the roots is a kitten, and peering into a hole their terrier stands quivering on three legs. Sometimes the father comes back with them. He has another voice with his children—he whistles, sings and with empty hands stares at the cattle feeding on the slope.

When the moon has risen and everybody has gone home, the heifers come to the hedge and you hear them from the lane below nibbling and chewing the juicy ends of the severed twigs. You hear a dim, large movement, like a tremor in the ground, and then you look up and see their heads hanging over the bank. There is a soft brushing and breaking as a beast looms away like a white-edged cloud, marked as the earth is marked by the moonlight. The trees and the wind and the beasts moving are the speech of the night, but the sky over them and over you is its thought, its being.

At night, or in the day wherever I am, by the stream, by the grass side, in the fields, my sight fixed near or far away, oh the mysterious throbbing senses which bring a leaf, a tree, a stone as close as my own heart! The frost fur, the flints embedded in the road, the elm bushes, the bird notes, they and myself are together, they and I, and my two sun-spirits, joyous and grate-ful—we are all in the moment. Life is in the beat of my heart, in the swinging back of a spray as a flight begins. The sky pours over and over, the sun shows on the hills. Forever the alders bud, forever over the grass the birds weave, forever the elms and the great master trees are beautiful. In dark indigo groups they disperse space about the fields, deep bare blue in the red and sorrel hills.

BEFORE THE SNOW

THE beauty and the tingling interest that is in the hazel buds, tiny as beads of coral tipping, and nicking the slender straight twigs. The catkins, the brilliance of the moss, the white birch stem, the ripple in the water. There is more beauty than the eye can love.

Let me feel the winter sunshine. Let me tell myself how it was in and of the bank like the spirit of white violets.

I stopped while a bird near me sang the meaning of the sunshine.

There was one dandelion in flower, yellower than yellow, blooming scarce an inch above the cart ruts.

The dust lay ashen as in summer; the haystacks leant up against the light resting.

Here by the four cross lanes I found out the primroses last year. A daffodil-yellow pollen of chaff so golden-rich as to make the land seem bleached has drifted out of the barn door across the pale lane and through the field gate. It·dusts the dry grasses and dead nettle stalks; broken straws cling to the blackberry trails, warming the hedge with the colour of the bright strands.

Oh happiness complete and perfect, illumining from within as this hedge seems to be illumined by the sun, warmed and cheered, coaxed from deadness to the first stir of life! Elsewhere I have called thought-in-earth a cord between us and what we see; but it is an opening, a rift through which the soul pours outward from us to join all in the world that is grown from light to merge with the universal atmosphere within and about the body of the earth and the sky.

Shadows narrow as grass blades separate the sun-lit surfaces of bramble and ivy leaves. The oak tree is bound around its trunk with the shadow cords of its branches: shade throws forward grass, and weed, and wheatblade against the very sun face. Leaf and form, wall and hedge, are floating on an understream of shade.

Standing on the hedge bank my memory brings the very smell of the flowers I found here, to my nostrils. Violets that smell of rain, the morning smell of primroses, sweet heavy cloud of cowslip breathed in a thunderstorm.

Looking across the field I see the lines of wheat, dark, bruised by the snow and frost, drooping over the little hard pellets of earth. The juice is straining through the narrow green blade, as a leaf injured by tight handling is stained by its own wounds.

From here, high on the four cross lanes, I see over the laid hedges, the great hills and the waves on which I stand. All is pale, but not faint, pale with winter drought, but clear and vast and beautiful, one tree behind another dwindling, with the fields hung on the sides of the hills like faded flags, and one great snow cloud and one sun inhabiting the sky.

I look long at this still cloud whose coasts even are not spreading. It goes with me like an image in the mind, travels with me, as I walk over the yellow-green pasture, like a meditation. It is perpendicular, not as a roof, but as a building in the air, all white and gold and grey. The cracks between the scales of bark around the elms I pass aren't more real to my senses, or in a manner more close to me, than the presence of the cloud. It moves because I move; it moves with me. It's as great as a town and the hill under a town's foundations; my stride through the field displaces it in the sky.

The short grass under my feet slips on the mud, and gives, as I walk, with the strain of my weight. The ground twitters with water. Stand still on the hillside, just below the rabbit hole, and it seems as if the surface which bears me is built over a stream. I stoop. I hear murmuring and flowing. The sounds are let out of the earth through the rabbit hole which is a big one, like a mouth, with a red tongue of soil lolling down the hillside. I put my ear close, and I hear the falling and trickling of water, the gushing and gurgling in the tunnels which undermine the hillside. The warren must be a subterranean stream with all its tributaries flowing down to the brook and alders at the bottom of the next field where the bullocks are feeding.

Walking along under the oaks which rise out of the hedge, quiet and leafless, I notice how sunshine is added to sunshine where straw and fodder is scattered in the sheltered places for the beasts. I see the fan of the branches opened, the birds flying through. I hear the rooks cawing, the woodpecker's peal of laughter where the valley narrows to woodland, the ewe's rich bleat, deep from her throat, prophesying lambs. The catkins are growing longer and yellower; they tremble now, and swing separate from the unmoving stem. Happiness, which dawned to consciousness by the barn on the hillhead, grows and grows, spreads through me. It isn't the joy of exercise, nor the happiness which comes with *pleasure*, from moving. Movement brings joy, is the delight of going out whether into the fields or into the town to enjoy excitement: but it is compared to this happiness only a fraction of the skin, a succession of swift and exquisite touches. The happiness I feel is like the sun rising into the clear sky and on to the fields, and into the cold green waters— growing and steadfast. As the sun, the feeling in me looks into everything and becomes everything I see. It melts the hardness of my body so that I walk free of knowing that I move. It is health, solitude, peace.

I see again the sun rising this morning, the sky veined like a leaf, in the east with red fire which trembled along its courses. Between the fir tree and the lime, the sun appeared and glowed whole, into the room where I watched. And then over the stubble at the back of the garden the longed for lark began to sing. From the sky down to the hollow stalks and the dark mole heaps the string of notes fell, constant and changing. In the evenings the thrush calls a rumour of green back to the hills, the blackbird whistles, the chaffinches churn their little pebbly songs, like minute springs dropping, but in the morning it is the lark I hear, going up, as the darkness rises from the roofs and tree tops.

82

Slowly, coming into sight round an elder clump, is an old man, shifting the faggot on his back as he grasps the top of an iron hurdle and prepares to get over. But he thinks he will rest first and so he is standing when I meet him, with one foot on the hurdle and knee raised, long sticks drooping along his back towards the hill bank.

'You're a good way from home,' I say from my side of the hurdle.

He smiles: 'I've been getting a bit of wood from this side the gorse. There weren't none last time I came, but I found more than I could carry to-day.'

'Heavy lot?'

'No-o-o. Not what you'd call *heavy* but awkward to carry. But I'm all right. It's lovely out and I've been sitting in the sun below that there hazel spinney most of the afternoon.'

He lifts his leg carefully over the hurdle and draws the other up with a groan of age. He is nearly eighty, a thinker and watcher of outdoor life, one who unconsciously tames and influences wild animals, who believes in the intelligence of trees and plants and flowers.

'I've been watching that cloud,' I say when he is over.

'Ah, thic thunder pillar. And I have too.'

He wears cord breeches folded and thickly clouted under a leather belt, heavy socks and boots, knitted waistcoat and a hat like a green anthill. He is always dressed so except for the hat which becomes an old trilby when he goes shopping in Ross on a Thursday. His hair and moustache have gone yellow, not white, and he moves with a yard of good ground between each foot—none of your narrow town walks but acres in his gait as he goes pushing himself along with his thorn. He lives at the bottom of a hill in a house very high at one end and very low at the other, with his wife and grandson. Over the tiled porch the eaves are yellow with moss. Down the path is a well, and the steps to the door go up higher than a juniper bush which touches the window sill. The garden is a square of whitey-green hillside, close bitten as by sheep or geese wired in and with nothing growing but the turf and a mud path sprouting thyme and moss. The rooms inside are paved with grey flagstones and implements and baskets hang from the rafters.

The old man has a pet blackbird, not a cage bird, but a wild one who has attached itself to him and sleeps under his bed. His wife told how she heard something shuffling in the bedroom and took the cat up thinking it was rats, only to find her old man's creature comfortably roosting for the night.

Most mornings he is to be seen going across the field to a dead nettle patch. With his big dry hands he folds the brown stalks over and over into bundles and then strolls home to light the fire with them.

The boy is thought to have a clever brain, and indeed his round green-yellow eyes are almost wild with intelligence, but if he lives to go to Oxford he will never take there such thinking power as is in his grandfather's touch, nor when he dies will such an understanding go out of the world.

How soft and golden the moss turf looks in the late afternoon! The tips of the mosses are silvery-green which makes the very ground like sunlight. Scattered by the hedgerows are the great bones of the ashes, great white splinters, where the heart of the tree has been ripped open for gate-posts. The places where they lie are like the feasting grounds of giant cats.

The old man told me how he had been sitting there on the steep hillside going down to the brook, resting there alone on his faggot of oak and hazel branches, smoking his pipe. He was seeing and feeling the warmth in the sun while the other side of the hill was blue in the shadow.

He sat on the ledge of the old wood path, once green with tree shadows and ground elder, now sunlit turf, old and soft under the hazel clump, half-way down to the stream. For hours he was there, speechless, breathing the quietness, seeing and enjoying and hearing all around him.

He enjoyed the smoke that came out of his pipe and distended in the air; he enjoyed the air that carried right back into his lungs the rare taste of winter sunlight on thyme and moss and sweet short woodland grass, with its flavouring of fresh water and damp bark. He enjoyed his sight, his hearing, the peace his knowledge brought him, the understanding of natural life. He took off his mittens and bathed his hands in the beams which were melting the moss—if he had been younger he said he would have taken off his boots and felt the fine turf with his toes and the sensitive arch of his foot. But he was almost as old as the oldest root under him as the greenest and most ancient round ant heap he looked at, and so he said, he did not expose his age.

On his left hand was the sun, the sky, the beautiful thunder pillar, below him the trees, the stream, the ant and molehills, the golden sunny turf, always above him grey hazel branches.

He told me of them all, not as one describes a place but as a time. He was away from time, not 'out' with it but in a different variety of it. The clock pendulums swing backwards and forwards in time; but in his variations of it the sun did not hurry and the cloud remained, and by them he existed away from indoor clocks.

There were the anthills, once mole humps taken over by the strong people of the earth and bulging under the mesh of grass and wild thyme and moss all along the outside of the ledge, not like excrescences on the earth's surface but like the sunken battlements of a castle wall, like green ruins gradually being smoothed into the contours of the land. Ancient, so rounded, so green with the vividness of moss after frost, they were lined before him like grass boulders. One tuft of moss was jewel-bright, the greenest flame in the earth around. He said he could have looked at it for a day, but the thought of the bees hovering over the pink thyme flowers in summer kept coming over his eyes.

He saw the gleam and glimmer of dead wood mingling grey with the ruddy yellow tinge of buds. He saw a hare touched with white bound up the plough land opposite. He told me how the stream sounded sometimes all along its length of bends and sometimes only where it flowed out from behind the hill.

The gnats were out in between the tree trunks like dust in a sun-shaft that could not settle.

The thunder pillar did not astonish him because he knew how close together are all the elements at all times.

He felt the gladness in the ground, and the still joy in the trees and the smoothing out of icy currents in the air under the sun's influence. Something that was knotted round his throat seemed to give way and his body felt room for warmth inside his clothes. He said he thought of the moles in their tunnels and the pigeons thinking of home trees where they were feeding on the greenstuff. And he sat looking down at the beautiful dead leaves and up at the great yellow-coasted cloud which endured. The air was soft—soft—the air itself was almost sunshine and gently moving as if stirred in a vast slow circle round the hills.

His 'now' lasted all one afternoon long with the thrush's notes, thoughtful with the trees. His brain did not tell him what he felt but it came to him straight from the touch of the ground from the height of the sky and the directness of the birds' descents to grass and bough.

His moment held him and the sun, the leaping hare and the shrivelled blackened nettle plant clinging to the roots behind him.

It held him still as he went back home with the faggot on his back, crossing the two fields and ducking under the wire by the oak tree. It held him fast against the swing of the pendulum on the wall when he sat down to take off his mud-laden boots, for the sun was still shining on the window when the clock struck an hour which a month ago had been darkness. For by eras the birds prevail, the sun stretches its course, the brain is illumined and dreams, thoughts and moods win the ascendancy over man and the universe. Though the clock struck the same hour and the weight descended the same number of inches, the still singing thrush and the sun on the glass cried that the mechanical hour was false.

The thrush's notes lengthen the daylight. The lark's song gives light before sunrise. The hour of his singing is a season to itself in the abridged year of a day. Lark and thrush are among the hoverings of time as it passes backwards and forwards naturally ranging and wandering through the universe. The idiot sway of the pendulum is no more time than the baton is symphony. What marks on a clock-face are there for that moment when the crow, tired of flight, droops his wings in the air and you see the lustrous contour of his back, the hanging pinions like blue-black leaves. It is only a second by artificial time, yet he *dwells* in the air—the eye registers him as something belonging to eternity. And those ages of minutes drawn out of the dusk when the thrush calls and calls again, shooting his polished rods of notes over the valley from his perch on the orchard branch. His music is fervent, penetrating, hurled as it were against the leading darkness—by what process are these eras reckoned, if they are reckoned? They should be, for there can be no complete time without them. They belong and are part of the true account: they cannot be worth just so many black strokes on a dial, or so many unconscious heart-beats, for that would infer the presence in the universe of a consistent watcher and listener to whom the beating, pointing and striking would be all that is contained in immortal life. No Omnipotence could be as futile as a pendulum, as vacant as agony. Besides, even then the mind of the singer, and *his* version of time, is left out.

Life is lived outside this penny round in a vaster and roomier circulation. We refer to the visible system only when our feelings are shallowest and our thoughts furthest from independent joy. The true time is the spirit in places, the era in your mind, the pleasure in your soul. It resembles your heart-beats as you know them, not counted one after another from birth to death, but occasionally rising to the surface, heard and felt as if your body *suddenly* possessed breath and pulsation. It is consciousness, but not consciousness of time. Rather it is the intermittent feeling of space, air, loveliness and life. The now is the time of all times. Migratory in humans when we see a whole sun in a whole sky and remember nothing of our age.

It was a pleasure, the old man said, to sit in the warmth and see all the things he knew about. The only long moment made of hours dilated like his pipe smoke on the air. The birds were never silent; the ewes bleated; the hare leapt over the furrows. Time began with its oblivion. Time was one thing, whole and yet divergent like a tree and its branches, a body and its senses, a sun and its rays. Happiness is as a beautiful house, beautifully calculated in a landscape. It can only be measured by the air and the light, and the flow of the created world around it. As a lovely building it exhales space. And vision which is only plain seeing and feeling, with intense joy added, lives in it.

JOURNALS AT DAWN

(To Pilot Officer George Francis Wadeson, R.A.F.V.R., killed in action, July, 1941, I dedicate these notes from my journals because he used to read them; and because without him and others like him there would not be any happiness in life to-day.   M.E.)

1939

. . . loth to leave such lavish dreams. Where are the Hash and Hang Company? What, or who is Thomas the Husband? And how did the brown-haired girl die who wrote a letter and finished it with the words—'my returning heart'? I woke, dreaming still—behind the furniture the figures moved, the white mountains—yet already it was too late for joy, too early for peace.

Another walk, aimless and inert. Turned things over in my weary mind. Frantically tired. Round and round the field, four brown hedges, square of sky, the oak tree that the wind licked. I found a pigeon's feather, sharp as a surgeon's knife. How beautiful!

To-day when I was out I reviewed my life. It seems strange beyond dreams that I was a child once, with huge days and nights. I with my stampedes of panic, my rushes, my despairs, my rolled up responsibilities which I never have time to examine; I with my prevarications, my debts to the seconds on a clock's face, I with my abused ears and shocked brain was a child; I so dazed and deadened, played with my sister in a meadow by the church. We rolled down the fine turfed green: the elms brought quietness to the landscape, the stream sang, rushes grew round the stones. And we had seen a snake in the wood. And I was on my knees burying a blue china bead in a molehill. There were hundreds of molehills with ants and sand showing through the

89

grass. We could jump from one to another. Foxes lived in the wood. I can feel the ground elder leaves—

Writing saddens me. Vision is turned into effort. Only in the *inner physical* eye is the radiance reflected. Life to me is solitude. Through solitude I breathe. Memory is solitude and seeing. My senses are all solitary. They desert me when I am not alone, or rather leave me paralysed at the point of desertion. I thought this as I turned into the wind. Leaning on a gate I looked up at the sky in joy of my loneliness. The earth was reared up against the tossing clouds. And as I achieved the stripped summit of the hill and my eye swept the vigorous lines, the spaced and wintry trees that made the identity of the place, I put from me the intermediate self and spoke to the spirit I, asking it, to what is it apt? The answer came by sight and by feeling—to the earth itself and not to the people of it. My passionate and only belief is in another order of being from my own: my joy is in the hills and the different notes of the wind, and the (to me) unbaptized stars. This feeling inspires everything I write or form—in a book, in a scrap of confession, as this, in a half poem, though hidden, it is the centre of the meaning. Do not the texts of the Geni always arrive at this acute summing of all wandering diversities? They seem to as I understand them. I shall be myself again, my old free self. . . . It was a most beautiful place where this interview with that self happened. The few and striking phrases in which the hills expressed the whole boundless solitude, the sky, the humanlessness, the wild-winged birds which cried as they flew, the black hollies massed against the wind, lent no inclination to ordinary company. But they fitted M—— who in some strange way resembles solitude. I could imagine *him* there beside me, silent, his keen eye ranging the skyline, his dark nostrils dilated. He has borrowed being with a casual gesture . . . he is a part of myself—all I know is that at some moments—as in that last stroll about the farm— we are blended in our surroundings, more than brother and sister, nearer than lovers, deeper and more unconscious than our separate selves. . . . I dug my heels into the hill. The steep sides made a thousand voices of my one—thousands of people shouted, the rabbits flashed to the furze—one burst from between my feet. Along by the stream I went, the boggy ground groaning under my boots. I stood in the middle of the stream and watched with a full delight the yellow brown and olive darting of the water. It twisted like an adder with the quickness of a snake: its cold little wriggle wound, broadened and curled away. The chill was distinct and bewitching; when I dipped my finger in it the water made a faint trilling and forked itself like a viper's tongue. I stooped—my broken hair almost floated—

Oh it isn't home—no—but it recalls the Mountain and Dad and those days when he was dying and I used to go out after sundown and watch the clouds crossing the sombre hill. It isn't home, but dearly it resembles a memory of home, and surely small streams have the most touching voices in the world? The breaks in the thrill of the flow, the sudden shocks of pure notes . . . if I stop my pen and listen I can hear the mountain stream now. . . . I love every grass of that hill, I love that ground.

Night falls, the roots of the stars. A load, a weariness. I surprised myself by uttering a loud groan. The dog raised himself and looked at me. One night I dreamed I saw a giant. He was sitting on the dim land, leaning against the sky. And again in the dusk an old man sat reading the Book of Genius, in a strange chaste room. And then the indefinite wraith of a dog which fled from me through vanishing streets, and when at last I caught it and felt for its collar I saw it had a brass plate engraved with Dead, October, 1604.

This dream I told and so spoilt it.

In the morning the thrushes sing while I am getting up and dressing under the grey slope of light. One leads them all, most beautiful and strong. Some days I think of nothing but those notes. Is he singing still, I ask, or am I only remembering?

1940

The light finds me at the back door, the frayed hem of my skirt brushing my bare legs, my hair uncombed. Stooping I wash my face in the bucket by the well—the sun flashes in the violent water, a spot of light like a torch ray, reflects from it on the wall.

I ran up the hill, I tear myself out of the brambles climbing to the top, to the sun. Up there I can lie down. My flesh is full of thorns, rows of briar tooth marks, sore and bleeding. But I heed nothing—nothing. I couldn't write about my thoughts if I tried. The light is queer—like lurid smoke. A green patch shines in that other heap of hills. Raindrops fall on the lichen, larks climb out of the brown bracken. Sometimes my book comes into my mind but more often I lie thoughtless in deep happiness. The birds, the flies, the bees, the sheep, pressing their nostrils into the turf, all express this happiness. Not one of them desires joy more passionately than myself. Or has it: neither book nor company do I ever bring here, to this complete solitude. No other person, dead or alive, is thinking or breathing here—except one, Gwendolen, whose 'life is in the beams of light, far far in the high wilderness.' In her I have created a being, a spirit who is my own and yet utterly beyond me. At times she is almost pure ecstasy, at others sorrowful with the sorrow of *places*, not people. Who is she, what is she? She died of hate, and now immortal she sings her freedom and her longing—for she hasn't rest. I hear her songs in my brain, but if I try to write them down they dissolve in a kind of *suffusion* of light, and I can't finish. Perhaps I don't want to, though poetry only comes to me through them. Full of passion and a remote joy, these songs seem very lovely to me, as I hear them, but written they stagnate: they were never meant to *last*, to repeat, or even to remember. I'm glad I forget them before I'm half-way down the hill.

On the hill all day, watching the bees and flowers. I was there from sunrise till dark. I wanted to see the whole splendid, lonely bow of light. But after the dawn the clouds grew stronger and darker hour by hour. The blue hills poured out clouds of scent and on the summit, flashed with a sinister gleam as if they were bewitched. The plovers flew over me as I lay by the stone. The light of morning touched their underwings as the sun rose, and again, in the evening, when their flight grew wilder, as if they swayed on an invisible storm. As I lay, ear on the ground, the sound of streams poured through my head, streams running under ferns, under hills, in unformed music, channelling the valley. I had no book, no poet with me, for who, after all, can be the poets of my own chosen loneliness but the plovers and the curlews, searching the sky? They flew and wheeled near and far away over the pale green fields, over the waterless brown vales where never a person is to be seen but only half-wild flocks, cropping the lean hillsides and lying out on the boulders with their lambs, over the dim air.

Once a ladybird came and rested on my hand, and I watched her in her tranquillity, I in mine, and the bees flying sideways among the bluebells. Yet there were pangs in me—a ghost. I don't know what it means, my love, nor what tongueless uttering I overhear, but it is true, my love, for these lands will make a ghost of me. Spring comes to the hills like a green light, all up and down and in between the motionless shapes, in and out tinging the clouds, the trees. Then the broom, and the atmosphere of bees, but the same sky and the same freedom. The birds they range. . . . Oh winter, my mind shows me your bare snow, barren lands, and yet how warm the grown grass! The thought of this spot is eternity, itself in all disguises. My country, my *body*, why must I die and leave you, why was I born away from you, why am I not your native spirit? To me the sun rises over Chase and sets over Garway. Evening comes and takes up all the sky. To-morrow is foreshadowed in the deep blue-grey clouds, folding away to the horizon, line on line; it will be a day like clear shade, still, distinct, and even aired, and the earth will be dark, intense green, with yellow flowered meadows. Darkness has grown like grass on this hilltop

The wind blows silently against the short stems, the tracks twist themselves. I am lost, I am found, the plover shrieks— I hear his wing shuddering, and I sit up in the green silence of grass and wind and dusk and think about things that aren't thoughts. I cannot understand how I am different. Whatever happens to me it is the same gulf, between me and this 'other life.'

1941

All the air is hollow. The cottage wedges into the south-west emptiness, the sky comes pouring over, the wind shreds the shadow of the lilac bush. I write my diary in the dark, it is 10th March. I have not written since I was married. I must finish my book: but for a few weeks I'll write of this inhabited hill. This is the true story.

The earth itself is a vision. I desire passionately to know what is in it, what animates it, what it means. Earth love—the grass, the fields, the rest at the end of the day when the sky is drowsiness, light and dark and that which abides in them. By the gate into the wild little field I always pause as if there were something there for me, waiting to be perceived, gathered and hallowed. I stood by the window in the moonlight, and the light was like dust falling from the sky. No, not from the sky, from the space above, for there was no sky and no sight, only a drifting downwards. I thought how closely I keep within the seasons: not possible now for me to think of the trees green, holding the nests in their fingers. If I try I get a false picture, done from a collection of memories—something typical, an academy 'summer.' I'll think and write of them as they are, wild, and tall, like giant weeds, against the rising of the moon, dumb seen through the glass but with all the gestures of drama. They feel, I feel. How much can we impute to them? I have a conviction of another kind of being groping towards me, as I towards it. I try to get at the meaning of my instincts but find it almost impossible. Perhaps to-morrow my faith will be shaped. It seems to me that I have been spelling words out loud, not uttering, not meaning them. I must remember that as I write the light is coming.

Washed kitchen, larder and parlour floors. Cooked, hung out clothes. Heard the plovers and the wind intermingled. The wind feels its strength and barrenness. Picked up sticks. The heifer in the stream, head down, hind legs up on the bank drinking the light in the water. Sunlight in the afternoon and the great branches suspended over the golden ground. The oak leaves lie with edges up, too quiet to glitter; then a gust, and look, myriads of scampering mice they seem, or fledgelings hopping and flying.

I got up at quarter to six. When M—— was gone I went to the door and lifted the latch and listened. The plovers were awake and wheeling but the rooks making a sleepy nestling sound under the hill. Down there it was darker. Blackbirds in the hedge. I went and fetched a fork. The shed let light in through the tiles and under the eaves revealing the belly of the roof. So softly, slyly the morning came without a sunrise. It was still until about midday when the wind came flooding the field like a river rushing back along a dried channel. It hit me as I stood on the path looking down at the shadows that had been so quiet but now seemed trying to fly away from the ground The movement seemed to be *under* them—almost as if the garden itself were quaking and bursting with some strange sudden growth.

Down to the farm. The sheepdog was howling in the granary, head out of the window. I fed the bullocks. They were all lying down. I carried the food in the basket through the fold. The chaff blew up into my eyes. One by one the beasts got up and took their places at the manger, quietly, as I scattered the food along. Their hides were hot from the sun. I carried home a heavy log and a can of milk. The pollen catkins hung in the grey bunches: small clusters of two or three dangled in the laid hedges where the supple saplings had been woven horizontally in and out between the living stakes. The splittings were like ivory chips: when still joined to the circular incisions they curled outwards like the petals of a full blown flower. Round here they call mending a gap 'glatting'—to 'go glatting.' In Gloucestershire it's 'sharding.'

Up the grey hills I slowly plodded home, towards the yellow sunset, near the ground. All was faint and sad and distant. Under the ash trees lay the grey spotted twigs and turfed molehills. Birds broke off their cold tunes.

Off goes the alarm—twenty to six. M—— lights the candle—five minutes to stretch and get used to my length. Somehow as I lie, covered, warm in the bed, the curtains across the window, I know in the first instant what sort of a morning it is. Full day at half past seven. The stones white in the dawn, the dawn like frozen water, dark with long whiteness behind it. Hoar on the sacks on the wall. The sun rose vigorously, streaming red down the panes. The mist from the melting frost on the glass made the rooms all glow. Now the ploughed field stretches all open to the horizon already clouded. Ch-ch-ch, hens in the farms and thump thump the wooden leg next door. A lark was singing in the middle of the sky. The clouds are coming—the wind screams like brakes—

13th March and no buds yet. How winter has leant on the land. From the hilltops you can see miles and miles of pale country: in the hedges grasses dead and withered, slack bracken, gaps and broken places, and yet green grass springing in the banks, like corn sprouting in an old basket. Plovers and rooks fly high: the nests are flattened, the thorns like dead rubbish. I went to bed early and read the old bird book which was my godmother's in 1866. It is of faded purple and gilt binding, with coloured plates of stone eggs suspended in space. The page on Yellow Hammers was gone. Yellow Hammers to me will always mean a walk with grandfather and myself rushing from bush to bush in shocks of anticipation unshamed by the calm figure in a black coat strolling behind me. I can still see through the lifeless medium of this stolid print the light that flashed from the flint stones on the field, their dark blueness, like thick glass where they were chipped, the seedling green of the corn they could not prevent, the sunlight, the yellow soil and the long brambles dipping into the grass. Oh exquisite, uncommunicable time! I was eleven years old then, on that day, my vision began. It lapsed: it failed, but it always came again, renewing my being, filling my breast like a fountain, opening my eyes. Lying in my bed not only do the bright images return, but their meaning and sum, the growing universe around the sun, its worship, its beauty, its glorious loneliness. That day was marked: sight began and I began, for the first time, to see that there was a Life which was not mine. 'There is something out of doors.' I said that to myself, but I could never bring my life to utter the words aloud. They sounded in my inmost being, clear, emphatic, inexplicable. I thought the wind was god — there was to me such holiness. . . . My blood flushes to the skin and my heart is *freed* by the memories of those first joyous pains! May! The Cuckoo in the hills, the hedge-grass high, blue with the soft rain, and the wild parsley growing tall, and the sheep, loud after the shower, thick on the green hilltops! As they were, they are; I love them for that I can never break into them, never know what spirit of life inhabits them. Only to guess that they are not of my fretful, wistful kind, sustains and comforts me. Comforts? Ah far more than that—*wings* me onward.

After a day's cleaning and cooking I went out. The ewes were feeding, the lambs jumping, on the short bright grass. They were calling to the flocks across the valley, throwing their lusty young voices as far across space as they could. One had climbed the hedge and was peeping down into the lane between the brambles. They are like moving twilight when all at once they begin rolling downward to the valley. There wasn't a person to be seen, but over all the land and sky a wonderful sense of peace and airy quiet. The hills were beyond words beautiful—dark and clear, only here and there suddenly tranfigured by the parting light, into a fierce nakedness. I saw the stream, lying under the green steep, under the gathering of the trees; it seemed as if it had stopped flowing, tied by the shadows over its dark and silver length. So strange it was to see its bend, like a narrow light shining from the deep hole in the earth up to the sky—cold and fixed, that I looked and looked and thought it like some windless perpetual dream of vacancy. The shadows of the trees and that dim drop hanging over the quiet field, the clouds that moved over the wild, bright sky, made the waters like a curved line of separate shining pools. It's lovely to walk along the high ridges, a swift step ahead of night, and feel the pursuing darkness at your back. It's wonderful, *wonderful* that the sky always shining, yet darkens to an inexplicable colourless void until at last the stars, outlined in the clear gaps, tell your mind of space unspeakably remote, turning the mental course towards infinity. The trees thicken about you: you alone are in the night version of the world: you think that no one else is out, for every sound you hear is Nature undisturbed. You are really changed, moved out of your place, a random wanderer, a discoverer . . . as you walk, you listen. You might be among dunes, conical hills, mounds instead of trees, their steep sides parallel with lines of stars. The deep air is full of low, soft, stumbling sound: the wind brings dampness and the cold dew of low places, and the ferny breath of spinneys and hedgerows. To-night it was like that; and before I came in I saw the North Star triumphant from the middle of the little solitary field that draws me so. I'd waited a long time for that moment—the star and, in line with it, the spot—the two, the earth and sky linked by my watching brain. How blurred the long grass was! How cold and searching its touch on my flesh! All these things began when I was a child. I realize now that I am re-living the first perceptions of my life, how I am interwoven with my childhood and how my beginnings are being uncovered, are *freeing* themselves from what I thought I was. How did I come to lose my being in the years? How could I bear to be a stranger for so long?

The woodpecker's laughter pealed out in the hot sunshine. Rapidly, madly, he billowed between the two hills, flying along the crack, under him the branches and the grey pillars. The mole city burst out of the hillside, its tunnels arching, crumbling, breaking the sod.

Carried my dinner down to the farm. M—— was just leaping off the hayrick—springing from the ladder to the ground all springy with hay. As we ate with our backs against the rick the sun shone warm and the breeze blew cold. A bee came swinging. Afterwards I sawed wood in the orchard and sweated all over. It was hard getting through those apple boughs and loading them on the gambel by myself. The old cider trees in all states of dishevelment tumbling and lying but still living in bushy twigs, knots and tangles, the blue-grey lichen lightening the grove like moonlight in obscurity. Sheep and lambs were in the orchard, and geese, and a cow by the gate with her neck stretched out and her nose wet, mooing hollowly for her calf. As I sawed some one yelled to me: I looked and there was a man waving his long thin arms over the hedge: 'Where's the Boss?' 'Don't know. I saw him in the fold,' I screamed. 'Find un will a? There's a yowe here needs help.' He threw up his hands and disappeared. No one at the farm but a doubled-up woman, smoking, wringing a cloth over the doorstone and the wild servant whistling, 'Who was it?' I hadn't been close enough to see. 'Why if it's Ken Bevan, he can do it as good as the Boss.' And she dashed out into the fields in hair net and gum boots, screaming, running, whistling through her thumbs, far away over the land in her blue overall.

Writing by lamplight. Dawn and daylight came before the moon set. There she was, round, yellow, misty hanging over the field, two elm's heights from the earth, and larks singing, entwining around each other's thread. It is real, it is real; it is lovely for ever. Brought my Bible to the door and read 72 and 73. 'The mountains shall bring peace to the people,' and, 'Truly God is good . . . even to such as are of a clean heart.'

Was able to put the lamp out at 7.30 and read. It's Sunday, but I won't go back to bed because my dreams are old old glimmers that will never brighten. A white morning, the air like muslin, wrapping a dark field. (*Autumn*? the blackberry bushes, the yellow grass.) Cold. Still. Birds whistling and chirring like little grindstones. The ring-dove winding the clock, sparrows, rooks, plovers and a thrush in the firs singing a whole song. Yesterday the field was harrowed. It looks as if knitted in a smaller stitch. I see it through the hedge, crawling away under the mist, land land land. The lilac bush is near, near, all its clefts, forks, twigs, buds.

Later, by the corner of the wood, listening. There is a difference between birds' singing in the woods and in the open, but *what is it*? I don't know, but I could tell it if I were blind. The difference is sensed by a subtle awareness of being alone— in the bird and the hearer—sunless singing, uneasy listening. Midnight in the sheep field—the earth dusky rather than dark, grass soft as sheep's wool. Over all the hills, nibble nibble and the gentle tearing of teeth. The North Star by the ash tree. The Wagon standing on its shaft. The wind sweeping round the shadowless darkness, a profound murmur. I remembered how the ivy leaves fluttered round the willows in the day, by the stream, and how a very small, almost invisible bird mounted, twig by twig through the branches, singing two little hollow notes. He was scarcely more apparent than a grey moth.

R—— has come. We were putting the car away in the field. 'Come in to bed.' 'Yes.' Yes. But I was thinking how I was alive up to about thirteen—and how vivid and pure and *true* were the things I saw . . . and did. Climbing the oak tree in the home meadow and singing right away over the field and the brook to Aunt Nan—why I could see the water running and the hoof marks in the sand—and existence since has been a smoke and a jargon until a short while ago when I found the same early beauty, as early still. Living with M—— has let me find myself entirely, let me go back, never I hope to be lost again, in that blind crowding.

My hand fell on the piano as I passed and left a dull smudge of sound in the room. It was ugly—*and* the dusty window panes and the dogs ripping their baskets. Cooking, hot and muddled under a storm. I watched for the rain. The queerest thing was that in this silvery copper gloom, I had a shadow. It was wafted up the staircase and along the yellow wall. And the touch of the chairs and table was icy cold. A strange day—the old eerie sound of voices. Reality is new to me. People were muttering behind the trees, crouching, and confiding destinies. Suddenly the talk ran to singing, hoarse, faint, then more gabbling, washed away by the rain.

But oh the coolness of the wet meadows, and the nets of buds stretched across them, and the thrushes this evening! It had just rained again, lightly binding the red dust of the fields. We put in the potatoes. Then in the late evening the walk through the quiet garden edged with the sound of trees. The bushes. The bricks of the greenhouse, the vine writhing against the glass, and the paths faint between the box. It smelt of rain-water tubs. Once more like a child . . . but only because this time is as *that* time. No going back but a long way forward—*nearer* to this resemblance. Good-night.

For many days and nights I've lived in my last dream. The *sense* of it was around me; the light persisted, and the darkness, which was light mitigated, like shade, will change soon and another era rise out of sleep. My sleeping controls my waking. The atmosphere of my dreams colours the sky, tinges this page, breathes from the trees, as my eyes pass up the paths. It was only that I was crossing the field and the corn was growing through my feet. In my hands were great loose bundles of yellow broom and gorse torn from the bare hill behind. That was all except the immense silvery blue mountains. Mountains of spring, dim behind leafy trees, a white mist smoking. Oh how strange it is in me, changing everything.

The thunder lives in the hills—they are grey—the sound is like their breathing and moving behind the rain of bird voices. To-day when I was standing quite still, feeling the light and air in every nerve, as though I were a small tree or bush coming up out of the earth, entranced by the inner touch of being, somebody shouted at me: 'Good morning, Mrs. Williams.' It infuriated me—oh it *does*, even more than an insult or a blow, that people cannot see one alone without charging into conversation. Never, never in all my life have I said to any one: 'Talk to me,' and never have I felt less like it than at that moment. The nerves of my body that had been like threads of perception, *whipped* me. . . .

How green and dark it is. Again the thunder slips, the cuckoo calls and the voices come slowly. The old men don't talk. They look at trees in a friendly way—old trees with horny bodies and ivy bulk. It's the old women: at the first word I hate them—at the last I'm strangely reluctant to let them go.

The lilac opens its yellow wings. Its shadow is a shallow thing. I sit here by the window of my bedroom, smoking, mending stockings, hearing M—— among the twigs, hearing the cuckoo's countless repetitions. I am thinking of Fanny on Hangbury Hill watching the moon float clear of the stiffening grass. But suddenly I am no longer angry Fanny in winter but myself last May, and all the Mays in all their cuckoo sameness and cuckoo loneliness, sound in my mind, and are seen . . . the chestnuts in flower, the petals of lime and wych elm, the sunlight that seems to quiver with life against the wall where the water reflections are like leaves of light on a trained tree. The last wide-open Spring-May, comes to my thoughts in its disguise of a country town. Dust, games, scrawled in chalk on the pavements, the gutter, the petals of May, a rocking chair in a back garden. The wind bends the smoke, rustles forth the amiable smell of lilac; pausing, the day waits for you to move, for the stately clock whose ticking is audible through the crack of a street door, to add another syllable to Time. You feel cool and free inside your clothing. You hear footsteps, a distinct thread of sound bearing down the street; a door knocker echoes, you turn expecting to see a *curé* in a cassock. . . .

In May the dandelion balls shine round against the green wheat. The stem snaps, cracks, when you pick it and the insect seed floats away . . . it drifts to the town and thereafter, wherever may be a broken wall, a crack in the stone plating, grows its glorious flower. The wiry, rushy, broom is waving on the hills, its separate sparseness massed in golden yellow clouds. Rush-like it dips in the breeze, dangling its weedy switches. I wish I were up there with the sheep and the small birds, less a person than a part of the air.

I am planting carrots. The thud of M——'s spade comes regular and hearty. Each time I go into the house the room is darker, the fire making a redder sunset among the chair legs. Tammas Cat sits on the post. Carefully he winds his tail up. The garden is fading, a background of wraiths for the speechless tree. Now the lamp is lit and the sky empty beyond the golden glass.

The next day. The world is so thin to-day: every sound comes through—as though a stopping had been taken out. At this moment of writing the larks are singing, the rooks cawing over the oaks (their droppings are like splashes of whitewash on the flowers), a hen cackling and the wireless singing through the walls, drifts over the wet corn. Music and rain—the finest rain that ever fell. It's like a web spun between sky and field. The far away bird voices are piercing by comparison with its hovering whisper. And now a bee and a fly—soothing, intermittent. The thump of a chopper, the plaintive sheep. The cottage is empty. To-day in a shallow gully overhung with shrivelled thorns and bramble leaves like bits of tin foil, and among the foxgloves I found the first bluebells. It was speckling with rain; with their wide-flung arms the trees held back the wind.

A flash of light and all the exquisite greens diverge. . . . Pushing my bicycle up the hill I stood looking at the roots of the hedge where the yolk-coloured dandelions had thrust themselves flat against the sunlight. And then I saw the little bird—a greenfinch—clinging to a grey hazel stub, perfectly still, and not moving a feather. Its eye, lit with a tiny white point of fire, like the star of its brain, was so unspeakably clear and intelligent, that it lent the whole creature, quiet as it was, a quickness, a trick of appearance and disappearance before one's captivated gaze. The bird itself was a grass long, shaped like a leaf for the wind, and designed for deception. Its wild being shone in its look, which it gave me profoundly, balancing, as it were, on its glance. Oh that fathomless opposite eye—what did it mean—what don't I feel, when I meet it? the shy, wild eye of that other order of being which shares the earth we think *ours*—shining, acute, impenetrable, the *seeing* climax of Nature through which the uncomprehended life peeps at us human exiles? What thoughts and sensations of water, buds, of roots, and growth and secret processes, he looked through that water drop of an eye, that spark of an enormous universal otherness! He was complete and compact: the sun shone round his tiny solidity, on the hedge and the grass and the dandelions. As for *colour*—I thought of the bits that drift on the surface of a stream— a scrap of catkin yellowish, a greeny bud, a petal. The hazel root was less than a wrist thick and yet his claws couldn't round it. Another moment and he was gone straight up into the air, leaving not the most faint quivering of presence, behind him. It has been raining—dark, spreading spots. And the lark singing to the cloud going. The violets were cold in my hand. The catkins have all fallen. I'm thankful these joys aren't my own, nor ever to be owned. People cannot reach my happiness. This summer I'll fling myself far out and swim the green hills.

The Pembroke Uncles and Aunts. As he talks I get glimpses of a sea tribe, their weight on the waters. Even the aunts with one foot afloat . . . salt, even aunty James with her carriage and horses, and grandeur—tarry hands put her there. Her white dresses! Poor aunty James. 'The last I heard of her was a scream from her deathbed as I went down the steps!' Uncle James was a master owner of a pretty little ship, the *Menin Bridge*. She had a funnel but was rigged. Uncle Dei got drunk and fell downstairs and died. His ship had three funnels. Seven sons went to the sea—the eighth lived on the extremity of land. They were all master owners. 'It isn't like that now.' And one somehow thinks of the sea shrunk away from the rock, and kegs rotting and the fuchsias gone to seed by the wall. They were all called by their surnames. 'Aunt James left father a family bible.' Or by their places—great aunt Bengold, aunt Annie Bengold—(broken off).

The may that smells of thunderstorms. Just to walk by it—just to see the cow parsley swaying, bending with rain!

> What have they learned
> the black pines in the night
> that they tinge with their sorrow
> the new daylight?
> What have they seen
> the mountains of morning
> that they give to the land
> so solemn a warning?

I *always* loved the earth. I can trace the germs' genealogy back, back to the first unconscious release. There was a wild, high field we children called 'The Mountain' pale, with long hollow-stalked grass where mushrooms grew and sheep pastured. It was and is the axis of the world to me. I would stand by the spring. The cattle had left their hoofprints sunk in the mud; deep divided slots (in Iceland I thought of those prints till they seemed before my eyes) that filled with water and shone among the rushes and kingcups. My feet felt under them the bending of the crust. I saw the dome of the hill—I saw it deeply in my heart and for ever. It was my religion to look, and to walk over the rise: watching it at all seasons, my thoughts began. Yet such thoughts are no thoughts unless the eyes, and the feet and the limbs are thoughts. But I have remembered, and whatever I have thought with my brain, I have forgotten. I never have forgotten the mountain shape and the mountain grass with all the air about it and the clouds and the sky between the blades. I have forgotten nearly all that has been taught to me but not the mountain to which I clung. The mountain was the middle of my earth, the parent of my life-consciousness. I clung to it.

I believe that a moment arrives when the spirit *must* articulate its faith. We know one another, we see one another, but it is as if we watched one dancing silently to the music in his soul. We don't hear that rhythm, yet to it the dancer forms his body. What song draws those limbs, and oh what ecstasy shapes the dancer's wondering smile? I have moved to my master air. I have thought, I have lived to the earth and the air which is the gift of the earth, since I was a child. I understand without words the thought that is in me: but without words what may be *testified*?

Lying on the grass in the still valleys, in the dark watching the rising and wheeling overhead of the great night suns, drinking the vivid clearness of the evening, sinking the shoulders under the clear cold water—floating, lying, standing, moving with life—I have become feeling itself. My simple being is thought. It was not necessary to learn anything, neither to name the stars nor distinguish the plants. I just could not be myself without them. They are to me portions of my body—my greater being. Why do I write this now? Because it is this great life that is steadfast. Remember that. Being and touching and seeing. Lying on the grass. Feeling your senses transposed to the things you see, watching your soul's delight take form and shape in the fields and woods, mountains and clouds.

As I write this the lark hangs over the silver dales. The sun is true, a white fire in the midst of light. I sit down with this book on my knees, and I put my hand, open, into a small grassy hole in the bank, to feel the moist roots, the living ground, the touch of earth which grips without holding. I feel all that I see,

entering and becoming part of my existence—the shape, the
colour—the black ivy trails, the wild strawberry flower, the
glossy lords and ladies leaves. The field from the hilltop sinks
steeply to a woody valley like a dark shadow sinking through
the silvery hills. At the bottom, a farm, old and sodden, settled
near the woods. All around me the pearly pigeons are feeding
on the seeds and all the swells and falls are rich with covered
harvests. I see the brown stream and think how the trout are
swimming; and I hear the rookeries and crow belfries scattered
over the land, telling me when I shut my eyes, how wide is the
earth here with its overlapping distances and its snake of water
fed from every field. Opening my eyes again I see the poultry,
like seeds spilt round the barns, see all in a few moments resting
on sight, and feel all, but above all the *response to seeing*—that
other life which is not myself but meets me and becomes myself.
How often lately I have used and thought the word 'earth.'
What does it mean to me? Life, the world, the beginning. Yes,
and the giving back of the force that flows towards me out wild
existence. God? When as a small creature I thought of 'it' I saw
'it' out of doors. I saw a running wind flowing over the dry
brown mountain grass, a field with no one and nothing in it,
steep and liquid with running grass and wind. 'It' the spirit was
there: I went to meet it and be merged in its being, but I knew
that when I wasn't there it was always the same. I lost it and
regained it—it was steady, uncompanioned, changeless—I was
fitful, restless, human. I lost it, until a year or two ago I thought
permanently, but then again at moments it touched me and this
time I want to testify. Going to the factory, going in buses and
seeing in the middle of my work the brown slight birds throw
themselves over the hedgerows like a handful of pebbles, seeing
the lark dart upward from the wheat and the white butterfly
hover over the sorrel, I've longed to put on record my joy in
life and *earth*. Somehow one creates in looking: one makes in
being. I feel a great strength such as the beasts must feel when
they stretch out and bring back a limb, such as a human knows
lying in the grass after swimming in fresh stone-churned water,

such as was mine galloping among the Icelandic mountains when the sun turned and whirled and swung like a stone in a sling over the pony's neck—I believe that this strength, felt with my body, is my spirit—

(Days pass. Once more I am lying on the ground against the swell of land but this time in the valley, nearer home.)

I have never seen such violets as these growing near me. They smell of sweet rain, but it is dry, mild and dim with a slow breeze. To-day I have cleaned all the house, made cheese, taken the dogs out, weeded the onion bed. The mending and planting leaves little time for writing. I have been resting. The plover piped, a rook climbed into the air, stretching his wings till he lay sideways fully expanded in the sky, in line with the slanting wind—and then down he slid on the point of his wing.

I look up from my writing, for a cloud passing has lightened the page. There is no sound, no rustle. I remember that as I came down I heard nothing but my own strides swishing the tops of the grasses, heard no footfall but only the pendulum swing of my pace descending the sharp hill to the brookside. I lay and spread out my arms. The ash buds are above me, and under the turf all meshed with yellow gold moss with grass roots like nerves binding it together. Sheep have been here. Their paths twist among the bushes. The brambles that swing over the narrow tracks are wound round with tight locks of wool. The mole city and the warren are near; under my out-flung hand I feel the dried rabbit pills, yet all is quiet here and empty, behind the shut-off wind. I'm tired, but the touch of the ground heals my hand, the growth of trees and grass freshens and renews me, makes me able to live the hours between walls. My brain and body survive, because I can look out upon the hills. I can breathe with my larger being, the visible, the vast sky into which the birds have soared. I can *be* the field, the trees—the movement of the branches in the breeze is like my own blood going through and round my life-centre—the earth is the lung by which I breathe—the earth is my greater flesh—the earth is eternity, and the stars begin—

THE FIELD

THIS morning, before it was quite light I walked across the meadows in the mist. I saw the sun appear, white as a morning moon, empty of power, its beams cut off. I saw the stubble patched vivid green where the clover is rising between the dead stalks. Then I came back. Strands of wet grass clung to my shoes. As I was taking them off I felt the warmth stealing into the air. A sudden shadow on the field formed the sunlight.

It is still very early but already the thresher is at work at the farm. People are fetching water, cracking faggots over their knees. They are bruising the dew, tearing and scattering the faint creations of the mist. Going to work they smear the dim grass with dark tracks. Their voices pass down the lane.

I sit down on the path with this bit of paper, the wall behind my back, the sun shining on my legs. The flight of the flies has begun; the white butterfly stumbles into the sun ray; crystals flash in the blue cabbage leaves.

The thatcher comes and leaves his ladder against the oat-rick. He tips his hat over his eyes before he goes up with a bundle of wheat straw under his arm. Slowly he stretches his arms out over the rick as though reaching into his clothes and slowly he begins his movements with his rustling hands. In response there is a harsh and restless sound: it is the last speech of the corn.

The corn is dead. Day and night for months I heard it, day and night it brought thoughts of the field into my mind. In the day its hissing made me dreamy, at night wakeful. Shadows and rain, clouds and frost, summer rain, and the wind dragging through it, I remember them all. When it was ripening I used to pull an ear sometimes just to feel the stiffening husks sweep the palm of my hand. If I shook it, it rattled like seed pods full of ripe seeds. The thatcher pulls off his coat and throws it down on the loose straw below. As he works the sun flashes on the buckles of his braces. The sheep dogs roll over and over, pulling a sack.

Sitting here where the sandstone crumbles on the path I listen to the starlings. They are gathered in a holly tree by the gate and they make a noise of bubbling and smacking, like wet lips. Only twice a year is there this thriving among them—at sowing time and again when the harvest blisters are drying on men's hands. Other smaller bushes are twinkling with what seems to be greyish dead leaves. It is the sparrows' wings. All along the hedge they are rising and descending, whirring to their perches on the twigs.

Over the field are pigeons and the great slovenly crows, drifting on a stroke of the pinion. The pimpernel has opened, the heat has shrivelled the cobwebs which were stretched like gossamer tents from each separate stubble to the ground.

Lying on the slope where the gorse blooms the vixen entices her cubs. The chilled snake lifts his head, filled with the instinct to sleep in the dark.

The sky is transparent blue, pale as a midnight summer sky when the stars are invisible in the universal enlightenment. Poised, the sun sheds its thin light over the field and the wall and the path, tinging stone with the warmth of flesh. The insects fly as with rapid thoughts. From the dying weeds, from the brick of soil bored by the worm, from water and the bark of trees hordes of winged creatures escape into the air. There are ladybirds, spiders, tiny parchment moths and great frail melancholy insects, vague as thistle seed. Frogs which look as if cast in rough gold frolic in the stubble. Every living thing seems bent on enjoyment, in exhibiting its beauty and strangeness before the killing cold comes to teach it death.

Now that the harvest is over the wind is shorn. Silently it ruffles the nettles, coming low over the bare field where leafless yellow flowers are trembling in the light. But it is never summer now in the mind, though the insects whine through the hot sweet air and the butterflies hover over the garden patches. A change has passed into the mood of thought answering the change in the Universe. The spirit of greater Nature in the sky and in us will not be diverted from the truth. There is a sense of boundlessness, a turning towards the sky with its winter outlines and firmer stars. The mind is greater Nature's—it is matched to the sky rather than the earth, which renews its prophecies as soon as the ripeness of its promises are proved and gathered.

Just now, even at the zenith, light is mingled with some quality of darkness. Darkness lasts all through the day. On darkness the universe is forming itself. A density thickens the sun's rays; at night the red of the sky is gloomy. The spirit of greater Nature in the sun, in the universe, in the sky, is in us and we feel, as no small life feels, the finality of a change which is imperceptible to many birds, and most of the fire dancing population of the air.

Soon the great bare wind will come, spilling the water out of the butts, whirling straws over the hedges, making people run bowed over the land like witches with all their claws out. But not quite yet. Ah how full of sunshine is the hen's silly cackling, and how genial the crows' gutturals! The morning teems with the noises of birds—not singing notes but just their life, conversation, movements, all careless of effect. The bird knows the beauty of its song; it chooses the moment to release it on the great enrolling wave of light or by the borders of evening in the lucid twilight. There is no chatter then—the ecstasy is never marred.

Last night I went to a neighbour's soon after it was dark, and returned across the field much later. I was watching the clouds and the stars, and I noticed on the first journey with what jubilation and vigour they shone, how fresh were the air currents, how strong and young were the forces of the night! The screech owls flew and the brown owls called with a beautiful clear note from tree to tree and hill to hill.

But by midnight things had reached a turn. The stars were wearing away by shining; their eyes were smaller, the breath of power was more remote, the flavour in the air was less sharp. Woods, hills, trees were silent and the pathways deserted.

Night and day seize the earth and sky with a giant's strength, a giant's delight, but after the first few hours they spend themselves and come to a standstill, waiting, with flagging vigour, to be dispossessed.

In the creation there are at work certain powers, movements, colours which seem to be different but which are repeating over and over again the same effect in different objects. All is continuous, connected; all is one perpetually breathing, changeless power; all is of one. The other day M—— and I were sitting on some mole humps looking down into a ravine of brambles and willows. He was watching the willows whiten as the wind moved on them: 'Look,' he said, 'that's the movement of the corn a month ago.' And it was—just the same lifting and swaying, the same tethered light, that we had seen so often in the field, transferred to the tree. We sat a long time and watched it coming down the narrow quietness of the valley, from tree to tree invisibly leaping across the dark undergrowth; landing the wind, like a bird on a tree top that moves downward under it, then springs back all the boughs up from the roots vibrating beyond eyesight. All the way round the steep hillside the willows were blowing up and down their height, like smoke mounting its own column. And M—— lay back with his head on a molehill while I picked hips and bramble sprays. Presently, I heard his voice speaking out of a trance of peace: 'Now the sky is the sea—when you lie down and see the sky going away from you, all the time flowing away from you while you stay still by the same things, it's the sea you seem to be watching and feeling draw away from you. There's nothing so restful . . . it's always going, and I'm always left behind with the same clump of grass and the mole hump and the bush.'

I often feel when M—— suddenly speaks like that that he thinks from inside Nature, that he has some thought with it, flowing with it. To go with him into the fields is to see farther than my own sight, and to understand without effort, from within. When we worked together out of doors, as when we were harvesting, he seemed of himself to create a harmony, like a third person whose presence befriended us both. He has thoughts, simple, in no way elaborate or strange, which he can make me see, as I see the birds and the clouds and the moonlight.

As I sit here by the wall I feel the continuity, the connection between all living things. All is real, in my eyes and in my mind. The sunlight revealing the grain of the world, the darkness behind the sight. The connection flows through all, from the thing in the hand to the thing in the mind, from the present to the vivid detail of some past flower, present in the brain. By me the olive-smooth seed case of the field poppy is balanced on its bare stem. I can feel its weight, see the black crest, like a seal, that shuts in the seeds, touch its smooth cold surface. It is like a deserted bird's egg, so heavy and cold in the hand. At the same time I see in me the hidden seeds in their pearly rows under the yellow olive skin, and the perfect flower all silky red and purple, tossing flimsily with the ripening oats. The actual thing I touch is not more real than the flower in me. The stubble glinting, the nettles bending are no closer than the sudden vision of the sword grass, seen so clearly, so distinctly, down to the sharp central crease which folds it to a point. I often feel as I walk by the trees that I see their roots with the grubs asleep in the earth, and the shiny chrysalis embedded in the rotten stump. Through all the connection flows onward, inward, outward, flowing life of thought, of sun and moon, of bone, and core and vision. As the stars are in the sky in daylight, as the sun is under the darkness, always in the sky, the eternal connection binds the universe, the transferring force passes forever from one life to another, from one form to another.

There was hardly a day or a night without some sharp, almost painful moment of perception. There was no empty time, no era when my senses did not fly to me with wonders. Like children, like five familiars they brought creation home to me, and did not know what they carried. I remember a morning so beautiful that on all the hills the men in the fields, the people walking, were looking upwards. Over our field a lark sang, over the same place, every morning as the light came out on the furrows. The notes hovered, never falling, but sounding in the sky where the beat of his wings was inaudible, the very music of the clouds. I see the tall elms turning red, their trunks being clothed, the leaves opening and I see the frozen field; I hear the rain falling into the green corn; at night the wind drew from it long sighs which reached into my sleep, and made me turn over as if the night were moving under my body.

The moon shone entire over the white still surface, casting a shadow from the cottage like a garden plot: midsummer midnight clouds rose from the still land tinged with the faint rainbow of the moon, the plovers flew and cried, the stiffening husks rattled by the hedge. I see the lairs the storm printed in the field, as though a herd of huge beasts had lain down in the corn, and I see the wind-blown cock scuff up the dust and walk away in the cloud of it, his feet plucking the ground as a sensitive musician plucks the strings of his violin. Birds circled in my vision of the sky, snakes sunned themselves, and men trudged over the land with all their secrets in them. The bees flew broadside carrying fertility. All, all in sight and hearing was Nature pouring itself from one thing into another, spending and creating, running like the wind over the body of life, and flowing like blood through its heart. All changed, and nothing changed. If I may keep this knowledge, this perpetual life in me, anybody may have my visible life; anybody may have my work, my smile, if I may go on sensing the thread that ties me to the sun, to the roots of the trees and the springs of joys, the one and separate strand to each star of each great constellation.

LOOKING AT A STAR

NOVEMBER. I am twelve years old, reading on the window sill in the fruit shed. I am kneeling on a wicker hamper, and my knees are numb. The daylight is cold and cramped. Rubbing my hands I sniff the air. The hamper is full of old newspapers and the atmosphere tastes of them and of pearskins and mouldy portmanteaux.

I have read myself out of existence. No such person inhabits the dark day; but suddenly I come awake with a rush of feeling. My crowded head feels suddenly clear, empty and airy as craning out of the window, I look hungrily around. This is real, I think, the colours, the brick, the ivy. It is as though something is going to be shown to me, once and forever. Things seem so *clear*; they seem to declare themselves aloud. My eyes have touch, my skin on which the air plays seems to be as glass through which I can look from every pore. Awake, awake to all, I know it is a rare moment, perhaps a beginning of a life separate from ordinary existence.

And yet what is there? The elm tree dropping leaves yellow golden all over, into the rainwater tank. They slide slowly downward on the point and settle with the faintest breath of sound on the olive surface. And below them, in the cube of water, like things tranced in ice are others suspended on edge and rotting. Then there is the pipe, and the grey cobwebs stretched across the corners of the tank, and then suddenly the bright shadow of the tree itself with all its stars of sky—lovely but gone almost before it can be lovely.

I lean out, sighing with the strange feeling in me. I can touch the cold sides of the tank; I feel as though I can touch with my mind the tree trunk, the hedge, the hurdle, even the farthest hill that I can see. What are all these familiar things saying so clearly? Why have I never seen them like this before? A moment ago they existed but quietly and without me. Now the leaves keep falling so queerly—queerly as though I had something to do with their falling. Something is happening which makes me able to say and know that it is true: 'I shall remember this. I shall remember each vein on each leaf. I shall be able to see this whenever I want to, wherever I am!'

I take a pear and bite it, and lean right out of the window while I eat it. Beyond the hurdle the sheep are feeding, their legs and ears black against the dull air, a smudge of red on their fleeces. One of them breaks away from the rest and moves slowly away to the feeding trough. How many times, I wonder, have I seen that movement in the dim fields? Particularly when I have been cold at heart, or foreign to my surroundings, or saddened to the very deepest sadness I can suffer by the longing for my country, it has come back to me. But the clear moment which was the prelude, oh, rarely, rarely have I had that again. Those are the eras, the visions, when the inner and outer meaning of the earth and sky and all that is in them, fit exactly the one over the other, when there is no slipping, no edge of obscurity, no groping. Ah, how impossible it is to keep those moments, to hold down for more than a single instant that joy of being oneself contained in all one sees! Feeling with the leaves, travelling with the clouds, seeing back from the star, into one's own breast that is the very essence of perception. It is then that one can live for an instant in the million kinds of life which fumble for the sun, or in the stars which search through space for the earth to shine on, and on the earth, a spirit to enter.

It is the strangest sensation for the mind to fix itself in the contemplation of one single natural thing; and one of its most singular phenomena is the amazing quality of universal perception which takes place in the thinker at the same time. Fixed on one, all things become supernaturally distinct and detailed. With the mind utterly rapt the eye becomes abnormally sensitive, but unconsciously, so that in recollection memory brings back a landscape where one seemed to see only a cloud's broken suns. Yet not always. Sometimes I seem to know each

separate thing while lost in the one, and then it is that I feel
profoundly the almost palpable linking up of the universe.
From life to life, from kind to kind, through the mind to the
sky and out to each planet, the chain reaches. Ah, who can
doubt it? Who that really feels what he sees can fail to be sure,
if he thinks at all of what his senses tell him? The air itself is felt
to be woven of threads of life. Even in the darkness they are
there. Looking up to the moon as it seems to rush backwards
across its own white hollow of light, looking at the sun's direct
rays on the earth, looking at the stars whose presence reaches us
through enormous darkness, who can deny the thought? Even
in sleep it does not leave me—the least thrill in the cord recalls
me, and in the morning it is there directly the day is felt on my
eyelids. Yes, even before I wake, I come to it. And there are
millions of spirits like mine. To them I unite because we are
still more closely connected. I believe in it. But I have failed to
describe it, because language cannot form the thought, because
it is wordless and unimaginable and pictureless, an inhabitant
unseen.

One July night I went out to look at the sky before sleeping.
The night compelled me, it was so strong! I walked along a
path between two fields, hearing the corn, which was high
above the ground, whisper down the length of its wall, hearing
the invisible sheep tearing the grass over all the still hills. Each
sound was distinct between the silences of the starlight, each
syllable of movement, and (for it was not late) each voice.
People were talking, men and women and children, in the
cottage bedrooms. There was something quietened, yet immense,
in their tones, as if they felt the sky in their rooms, touching
them—as if the roofs were gone from over them, and the pale
tingling blue of space came down to their being. Down to the
valley, surging, seeking, rolled the sheep, past me and then
there was left on the bare grass, on the horizon and the tree tops,
the power of the stars. Their breath was in the air, a thrill, not
cold but cool, like dew. I tasted the stars; I felt them in my lungs,
in my throat, and on my eyes. They shone from star to star

across all the sky and down to earth. I felt my way to them by listening and by touching what they touched. The long grasses on a wall were each distinct and clear, clashing their feathered heads, and the leaves on the bramble sprays were separate shapes. It was like a perpetual dawn. On a level with my feet the grass hill suddenly swerved to the valley. Before me shone a glow of purest light, paler than any tone, fainter than the faint thrilling blue above. It was the outermost ring of the sun, down below the earth, part of the curve of the sun's furthest circle. Above it, in the very forehead of the east, showed a small star, as a separate speck, apart from all the rest. On it all the mystery in my thought and sight became fixed.

At first it was as though it was beyond a moving transparency. I seemed to look at it through a clear current of water. It seemed to swell and shrink and to be misshapen by some intervening medium. And yet it was always the same . . . not splendid, flashing, or placid, but soft and alone, and full of a gentle vibration. The depths about it were grey where the blue waned above the sun's influence, unlike the infinite blue and violet around the great constellations in the zenith. It lay where the shadow of space lightened towards earth, closing finally around the curve of my hill . . .

I looked into it. Behind me the south, shimmering with white fire, the grassy path, were cut off at my last stride. Though I could hear the breeze in the oats, and was conscious through and through of the long hills, like wings bearing the earth's body through the air, and though the awed voices still sounded through the windows, yet there was only the star and myself meeting. I saw it with my heart, as I sometimes see my hills, and I knew myself in it, and it, from space, in me. Deeper and deeper it touched me, so tight drew the cord between us it sang! The song gathered, the string, feeling the music hummed, but as the breath came down upon the note I was obliterated.

THE AUTOBIOGRAPHY OF AN AFTERNOON

AT two o'clock when the sun went behind the clouds I had my dinner. I ate it in the kitchen, sitting at a corner of the table in a draught because I needed to be quick over it, and because the moving air prevented my thoughts from settling in the house.

When I'd finished there was only a cup to rinse, and when that was done I went out into the garden again and planted a row of onions . . . late ones. Then, as soon as the sun came out and the dark fresh earth began to fade till the raked seed-patch showed grey crumbs like ash-dust, I collected my tools, my rake and hoe and small fork, and leant them up against the hedge ready for the evening's work. Familiar was the feeling of the three polished handles gathered in my hand as I stood for a moment pondering on what I had done.

I called Gladys, and carrying a basket and a couple of sacks to lie on, walked to the hillside which they call 'the Gorse.'

It seemed to me that any spot would do for me to rest. Any place, as long as the sun would warm my bare legs. I started with dependence on the sun. If that deserted me I must go home and plant again. Any place would do with the grass and moss under me and the tall broken dead bracken around, and the company of domed anthills. But I chose this faint hollow in the hillside because I have lain here before and I like the forms I know. Grasses become individual if you look at them long enough. Besides, a pair of wrens was courting in a blackthorn bush and the sound of water was delightful in the narrow valley.

This is the story of what was around and within me that afternoon.

Bit by bit and sense by sense I began to be profoundly conscious of the place where I was lying . . . the smell and heavy goldenness of the gorse bloom, the different *strands* as it were in the tiny waterfall below me, the bracken canes and

stones and weeds and brambles. A ladybird and two spiders
sunned themselves on a ridge of dried mud but my closest
companion was a woodlouse asleep on a large dead oak leaf.
There were brown butterflies with turquoise studded wings, all
cindery black underneath, beating about the anthills, and the
droning of bees in the sallow trees.

All these minute creatures were aware of me and communicated with me in a way that I can hardly interpret. They
did not flee, but rather sought me out as if soothed by my
presence. To me they brought a sense of permanence, of
reinforcement and reciprocal life which I believe they shared
and understood.

The things I see are the things I think. I passed my first hour
looking deeply into my surroundings, touching them with
hand and eye and mind. These grasses and dry, hard crackling
leaves lying on the ground, these bushy pollenless catkins and
red-brown lacy fronds, these clouds and sun-spots in the sky,
they are my thoughts. Entering me they collect an intensity of
expression, a separate yet coherent state of being which is
universal. We are contained in the rise and fall of earth, in the
smell of bracken and water, in the air and the space and the
depths of light we cannot plumb. I feel that the pale-blue sky
covers our common essence, hides the dark purple of infinite
light whose shallowest shallows only shine around us as faint
daylight. The white stars are covered, and the dark store of
endless noons too far to guess at; of that bottomlessness
above and the blind depths below we are made and know our
parentage.

Very gently I drew close the oak leaf on which the woodlouse slept. It had exactly the grain and surface of calf-skin when
it is stretched over the boards of an old book. Its veins, from
which it had shrunk, were raised like cords. At the first glance
it appeared no definite colour at all but a residue of natural
brown, pale greyish blue and white. At the second it was even
less distinct and recalled only age and wearing away as if only
by chance it remained. It was beautiful, but if the hand had

stroked it as it longed of itself to do, it would have ceased to have been an oak leaf and become sun atoms, or the shadow through a rainbow, or part of the moon's aura. The woodlouse was a deep violet slatey-blue against it.

The ground growth under me was the same colour as the sacks I had thrown over it. Thyme, moss, grass and bracken canes had been woven by the winter cold into a thick, dry and springy mat through which the bright new grasses were thrusting their sharp blades. The bracken was broken off about two feet from the ground and the splintered cane hung down by a split strip snapped probably by the snow.

I broke a cane to find out if I could smoke it. The stalk was porous with long needle length cells, like biscuit, but it would not draw because there was no continuous passage of air. Trying, I made a discovery—the pupa of a fly inside the stalk, wrapped in its opaque shawl. I recognized it as a fly because the body showed through the shawl in which it was sleeping and being made. Less than a quarter of an inch long it was marked with shadowy rings. The eyes were not developed. I had killed it by laying its shelf open to the sun. Perhaps light in a dissolving flame burst as a dream into that dedicated trance and with awful pain the creature, half grub half winged fly, died in premature contact with its world.

The presence of the pupa in the tiny chamber of the polished bracken stalk raised unanswerable questions in my mind. How did the grub reach its present niche? There was no continuous passage through which it could crawl up or down, or which would allow a fly to get in and deposit an egg in one cell. And this one was not a broken cane—I had touched none that was. And why should I have split it at the very place where was the cradle? I tried several others with no such result. As far as I could experiment I had by chance destroyed the only pupa in all the bracken around me. It made me wonder what other hidden thing lay close. I had a kind of mental conception of progressive sleep through and through the burr-like hill on which I lay— an idea without definite image because never seen. I knew the snakes were sleeping. And the fronds and buff grasses and wild brambles hid the mouths of a thousand holes. The ants were under their green dome. The bees and the butterflies were full of mystery. What else, what else?

Even as a child I could not look at a bird or a last summer's leaf and say, 'This hasn't anything to do with me.' When I touched a grass stem I felt in some strong way united to it. When I swam, when I flung myself down on the ground out of breath, when the snow touched my bare hand or the wind made its way through the window and breathed across my face, I instantly recognized an old old allegiance. And so it has been ever since I can remember, lapses and then true moments, vivid and telling. I shall not forget the pupa.

While all this was happening there persisted in me a distinct mind image to which my conscious brain gave no attention until long afterwards when I recalled it. I saw the lichen-like chrysalis woven in the corner of our kitchen window. I saw the great sealed eyes like frost smeared glass and the powerful sprung legs through the thin case. If I had held it in my hand it couldn't have been clearer or more detailed.

While my eyes mental and physical were thus occupied, and my mind was hovering close over the earth, my hands of themselves were thinking and wandering, feeling the brittleness and smoothness of fallen leaf and hard dry stalk, reaching out from my side and touching the nearby track where the dry cattle-prints showed like half moons. The oak leaves had been swirled by the south-west gales far up the hillside and I had been crunching them unconsciously in my palms. Now brought all at once together I noticed how they weren't decaying round the edges but falling through themselves between the veins, leaving queer cellular holes. It was absorbing just to pick them up and look at them and see the high light making them lustrous. The bracken fronds had no high light or lustre but were only patterned dust. They had coarse teeth like a saw and pinched to nothing between the fingers. The oak leaves looked somehow infinitely older than the tree which had shed them.

Shutting my eyes I became the thought of what I had seen. Not a part of my body but has its brain. I meditated and received my meditations throughout my whole solid being. My brain was like the earth in which is my most ready world; but worlds more beautiful and more beautifully conceived are in the air which touches me all over. The brain is the earth, the body is the universe, strung planet to planet by impalpable communicating threads.

Keeping myself close and still I thought how lovely it was to hear the sound of the stream pouring over rock, the delicate wheezing cries of the wrens jumping from twig to twig. I pictured the stream being pulled forever from out of the sunlight into the bushes. It seemed to me that I could distinguish the sound which was the smooth water and that which was being forced up as bubbles from under the waterfall. Even the ripples which washed the bright moss were audible, and the slight swinging of the twig tips as oak and hazel touched. They held their branches out into the pale evening blue sky. . . . My senses were not exclusively fixed on anything: they wandered up and down receiving their own precious thoughts and impressions. Rooted in me they were growing outward like the oak boughs whose buds live a sensitive existence quite apart from the feelings at the roots. The roots lift and heave; the twigs feel the buoyant air under them like a raft and the sun drawing them out longer and longer until they feel they must shoot like arrows into his breast.

The oak buds uncurling brush the sere hazel catkins and feel a different life from their own, meeting and touching them as I feel an infinite store of life meeting and merging with my body. There are the thoughts in my mind and the thoughts in my body, the thoughts in my nerves and those in my eyes, ready to meet and mingle with infinite thought as is my breath to mingle with infinite space. When I describe what I see I tell what are my thoughts, and what my mind will be to-morrow. I turn my eyes to the sun, the sun which faces all things. He hangs in the sky, suspended between two tall clumps of elder and hazel and thorn. Under the branches the sheep are lying, for this is where they go when the turf becomes too hot and too like another fleece pressing against them. The hazels glow. Their catkins are the wicks on which the sun kindles his beautiful illumination. All around me the air is full of the burning insects flying. The big wild bee is like the heads of the flowering grasses Sian and I called 'Knights' . . . the swarming ash flowers under the bud resemble populations of insects, the tortoiseshell butterfly is a free, untethered breathing flower with glorious and brilliant sight. Yet I don't imagine the *rooted* flower to be blind because it has not those transparent eyes. Is light without perception because *we* grope when we are blind? I imagine there are few people who don't instinctively feel that the sky *regards* what it illumines. The moon, the sun and the stars, who of us thinks of them as blind because, rarely, they clash together? It is possible to conceive an idea of sight through the material of which all visibility is made—to think of one great combined sense in mere being, by which a flower or a tree receives more diversity of vision than a life-time of eyesight would give to me.

One person, one plant, one of anything, lives infinitely. *One* lives *plurally*. As I, looking up into the pure and wonderful sky, remember last night looking down from the window and seeing the white daffodil in the twilight alone, blissful, its petals, stem and leaves trembling, lived for a moment in its beauty. . . .

One is in everything. One lives throughout the universe and beyond. Though I think what I see I don't see with my eyes alone. Never shall I see Nature passing without falling in with its order, myself mixing and coming to consciousness in all life.

All existences merge, even physically. Things more than resemble one another, they are more than kin, they are one manifestation. Likenesses are symbols. How should we *not* grow like one another when the same element brims up in us all, when we ourselves are conscious sometimes that our separate existence is an intermittent form assumed, we cannot tell *why*?

The life which is opposite me, be what it is when I reach out to it, responds to me. There is no picture, no form of life; and in no form but as an unseen element, it floods the earth and sky. As nothing individual it returns. As nothing individual I go out. Lapsing and losing myself I seem to breathe through distant trees; to look around the world from stones in the fields, and down on it from the budding mountain. It has seemed to me that ever since I was a child creation desired me as I desired creation. All of us sought one another. The sympathy I longed for was not human sympathy, nor any human idea of it. It wasn't tenderness I wanted, nor mutual recognition, mutual pleasure; it was nothing I could describe in human language. I call it reciprocity, but that is apt to be too much. The further I can get from being a human being, the clearer can I feel in me the idea of an elemental conception. I *need* to feel it and have always needed it. I need and desire an extension, a plurality of being. If I am still, the birds and insects come near to me. Sometimes I could almost imagine that for them our shadow enriches the ground. Why does the butterfly hover over my hand with all the yellow gorse to choose from? Why don't the wrens fly away? Among their tremulous movements is a quick turn towards myself; their eyes seek mine. As though in their breasts aches the same solitary instinctive longing for abstract communion as does in mine. They and I seek the other version of the same. Solitude is this, and mystery and prayer.

I don't wrap myself in solitude, I go naked in it. I discard my particularity, I discard myself. I don't want other humans to be solitary with me because their humanity on top of mine is too much for impersonality to discard. Through the multiplied wrappings nakedness cannot emerge. One lava to a chrysalis! There is so much of me in any company of my own kind, so much the more to throw off. But every feather of a bird takes a feather's weight from me, and with every leaf and blade of grass a leaf's ponderousness is lifted from my nudity.

When we were little my sister Sian and I had solitude together. Mutually, without a word being spoken, we knew the significance of certain places, certain trees. Names which meant more than words alighted on them, names which neither of us ever seemed to invent.

How wonderful it is, how beautiful! This sky expands and expands, blue beyond blue. There seems no cloud, no night ever to come. It is the foreshadowing light of summer's never-dark, the gift of eternal presence which is the mid-year's. The crow sheers off a corner of the blue, the blackthorn bush balances, weighing itself by a bud now on this side now on that. Oh that I could tell, oh if I could!

Suddenly I know where I want to be more than anywhere else. I know it as Sian and I knew which play place was the day's, without discussion, without choice.

The touch of leaves and flowers goes with me, cool and gentle. The sky grows vaster and paler as I climb the hot and slippery path. The single isolated sallow is hazy with bees. They move all over it as if they were its outermost flowers, and the air near it is palpably whirled by their wings whose sound seems to raise the temperature. It is a tree perfectly domed, with a single trunk, one great bunch of yellow polleny blossoms. Curving around its curve is the clear sky—just such a still and *dwelling* expanse as prepares one to see stars dawning, and yet to be surprised to see them, as each pricks the eye . . . it's afternoon, yet strangely this is an evening sky. It makes me remember the end of our green games, and coming back with Sian from the meadows with a ball in my hand, to be given bread and cheese on the step. The dew stars are over us, the growing grass is deep and cold, with sorrel in it and silver dandelion seed. Our feet ache in our wet shoes, there is not one moment, one degree to be added to my lovely day. Oh what Perfection am I taking in to sleep with me? And how did I *then* understand its rarity?

As I wind up and along, around each other view the corners of the hills come into sight; valley joins valley, stream joins stream, and the sun swings gently behind other trees. The walk is short, but it seems a child's journey, endless with detail, eternal with imagination and freedom. I had nothing to do; but what does it matter that usually I *have* to go to and fro? The more I move the freer I am. The sun has an errand. Let me run mine with his. I'd rather pick up wood and carry water where the heavens work around me than be cheered and processed by a working multitude. I hate, not only a crowd, but him who makes it. I'd hate a life of bellowing and bowing. I hate obeisance and idleness called privilege. I hate the smoky djinns. I'd hate to make a saddle of my neck; but I would not refuse the *brief* load. It's freedom to me to carry away with me not only the beauty but the bounty of trees. I love to fetch for our needs when they take me out of doors, for I have made it so that there are few *necessary* errands I go which are not mental and beneficent as well as physical and pleasant. I love to be *needy*, because it gives me so many uses for my liberty and so many opportunities to enjoy it.

This very morning our tap stopped running so I had to go down to the brook for water. After I had rinsed and filled the buckets I sat down on a stone in the middle of the flow, and watched a pair of chaffinches who were playing together on the grass by the edge. At least a dozen times they perched themselves on a sharp-edged rock, twitching their tails over the water and looking at their pink breasts, all within a couple of yards of me. Then came a third, and after circling round one another, showing their white markings, they all flew up into a willow and cheeped.

The stone rocked and by moving my body I could make it churn on the pebbles underneath. My knees were warm in the sun, my feet were in the clear, cold water. There were a thousand lovely and interesting things about me—the green light of grass transparent as if a subterranean sun shone through it, the golden stones under the water, the voices and the shaded ripples. I did not stay more than ten minutes, but long enough to see an adder come down the bank, and hear the ring-dove purring far up in the elm. The trees are her green mountains—how happy, how peaceful she sounded in her steep pasture! And I love the viper . . . years ago I found out that I loved him whom I had always feared, just as I discovered music which I had not heeded. By *loving* I mean I am intensely interested in him, and deeply sympathetic, and profoundly stirred by his beauty. He is marvellous, salutary, innocent and bright, without a slur. I admire him with all my being. It is a wonderful day to me when I see him. Since I lost my fear one more hard side of me has been opened to the universe. Therefore I feel grateful and humble towards him, and timid with a timidity which is not afraid.

In the summer there are many vipers on this hilltop. They like the short, needle-stemmed grass, the nearness to the sun. This place is like Nature's hearthstone where she has set herself to stitching her most minute designs. Tiny grass, tiny flowers with shallow roots, minute insects toiling with grains of sand. A place of small petals, white and blue and yellow, so pure and intense in colour and texture that they seem to touch nerves more exquisite than those of the eyes. Small plants, small anthills, and large echoes, faint and long, of the wind and the cuckoo. Only the ground and the sky *shaded* by light, and the intermittent humming of bees. I call it the South Bank. This was where I wished to be when I thought of Sian: this, when we were children, would have been one of our dear significant spots, only to be enjoyed at times which made their own communications to our understanding. Sian, do you remember —how dearly do you remember?—the Mountain, Meredyth's Field, Katy's Meadow, the Bank, the Gap? *You* are the rhyme to the word that can't be found. The names are almost nothing —they only point to another name within, and another and another, deeper and deeper until *instinct* is touched. A name in a name and very far down inside us an idea which two children had of what it all meant, and the *reason* for coming to-day.

Every sound but that of the bees is far away upon the opposite hill. I hear a roller jingling, a lark in the sky, a boy whistling as he rouses the cows from under the trees where they were lying. And the cuckoo. Only the last of his two syllables reaches my ear, but the unheard note is *felt*. '. . . ckoo, . . . ckoo.' Land

and space are in the missing beats. It's thus I hear him on a cloudy morning when the new leaves have just found their rustle and the yellow of the dandelion flowers joins over the green. On a dark silvery morning, opening a window, '. . . ckoo, . . . ckoo, . . . ckoo,' the echo of silence and of valleys changed by grass. You cannot call it a song. It is more like a chant, coming now and again through the air, as rhythmically unheard as heard. It's a strange thing to me that the vernal poets whose bird particularly he is, seem never to have noticed this his most usual incompleteness. With them it's always the 'twofold shout.' Really the voice of the cuckoo is as sunlight on a restless day—what you are not getting, somebody else is.

I feel, oh so joyful, sitting on the grass and listening. That cry is as precious to me as the mountains. And the whitethroat's dip into the patch of nettles—it seems to me the profoundest action on earth. Like a visible breeze the sulphur yellow goes floating by me, his mind in his flight. Beyond him but far down shine the daisies in the meadow, the grey orchard bloom. The bees' humming is alternate—the wild bee's sweet thick 'zum, zum,' and the shriller buzz of the honey bees. The wild bee is working close to my foot on the ground ivy flowers. His orange poll is like a clot of fire . . . you could follow him home in the dusk. We are all of us here in a calm which is a creation by itself. From tiny dots at the bottom to big smooth humps a yard away the anthills are rounded against the slope, each with its dark side away from the sun. Bird shadows, transparent as leaf shadows on a window, glide over the ground.

There's nothing I would not give to retain this which is all the meaning in life to me. The freedoms, the immortal light which the lovely season offers, extension, greater and more boundless perfection, is held out to me. At night there is the moon shining straight in on me, and I feel a thousand openings converging. In the greenish aura of its light mingling with the clear pale blue of the sky, it is to me the same moon which lit the meadows when we children were going to bed with the smell of the whole growing world in our nostrils. The same moon and the same season, the same green above and below. The time is identical. That which drew me home again to perfect light sleep, like dawn, draws me still. Sitting with my head on my knees I see Aunt Nan's garden and her flowers, the yellow cactus, the trefoil that grew in the greenhouse floor between the bricks. I remember dipping water into her watering can from the tub by the cornflower bush and the bank behind, and the apple boughs dripping on my neck. These are things which I thought only I *knew*, but which the youngest bud retains and repeats to me year by year.

DOWN GREEN LADDERS

THE Spring is coming—going like a lifetime spent learning and forgetting the body's exquisite arts. Suddenly, while I write, this room is filled with the sound of a gentle downpour. And the light stoops under the rain forest, hemmed in by the quick shining stalks which slope across the window.

Softly I go upstairs and open all the doors that this magic breath may circulate through all that surrounds me. And softly, with ecstasy in my heart, I go down the path to the iron gate where the celandines are furled in the grass, their bronze-backed petals blending with the green prickling hedgerows. Oh the rain drops freckling my face, the buzz of a bee mumbling the wet red dead nettle flowers! The sound of the rain streaming down, how beautiful it is! How beautiful the hedge, the brilliant field, the trees and the sky! They seem to run with wet colour and dye the air with an earth bow!

Indoors, the wind swings the curtain and puffs the damson petals along the sill. A dark sound fills the room. And I feel so happy, with all this to myself. Not to break a sound or lose an interval, in speaking. What joy, what peace and contentment!

Then the rain thins into lines of brightness dropping past the sun, and the blossoming orchards are all curdled green and white. The doorstep is wet, the path black. I should like this morning to go on for ever.

In bed last night I heard the rain. It stirred the earth like a breeze, with its falling coolness. It told me of the grass, and the soft surfaces of field and pasture. Its murmur was only the faintest overtone above the unshod sounds of night on the sheep-turfed hills, only just louder than the running of the stream whose small stringed music seemed to carry a vast impending symphony held in a dance, tiny and huge.

I lay listening, while the flashing needles split on the black panes, and the earth met the rain with corn and leaves. There was the flop of water flouncing in the butts, and a wild, blossomy smell, the more perceptible because in the darkness I was less aware that it was an invisible delight.

My life brings me visions by day and by night, but most vividly when the rain falls through leaves with the lark's voice, or when the clouded sun suddenly brings out lustre on the grass. Then every form and image sensed has an inner meaning. And it stays with me while day and night pass quicker than the time they bring. The days and nights go and leave their hours in my breast. I can go back and be in what I have seen. In the dark I can see birds in all their instantaneous actions—flying, mating, like balls of whirling light, stooping to peck at the ground. I can see flower forms under my shut eyelids, and countless corn pouring away whole fields.

Perhaps many will not believe, but there are days when one lives alone bringing such a sense of the single odd, original life given, that it is almost impossible to forget all one owns in existing. The rain says quietly: 'Look, listen, open.' And I want to open everything—my house, my eyes, my hands, that the dense green atmosphere may penetrate to everything that touches me . . . that every part of me may feel. My prayer then is for an empty mind that nothing stale, no old thought or discarded entity can come between me and my new sensations. When the storm is over and the last drops are dripping from the lowest leaves, and the grass glitters and an oily wave rolls over the wheatfield, then can be felt the subtle presence of a fresh earth to be understood.

After the rain I am a stranger. I have not seen these trees and clouds and glossy grass before. After the rain the blackbird sings, and with a fresh understanding I must listen to the way he does it. He sings to one direction, listens to another. He sings not to the ground under his tree, whose green blades enclose the flower colours, but to the hill a mile away. To him it seems the earth is first and foremost the only enduring reason, the closest joy. He sings to the hill as if it were more real to him than anything that happens to himself.

Later. I was listening to him, as I sat on the valley side under the living and close by the dead ash tree. The living tree was in flower and its branches flowed. But the dead resisted the air, and stood, its bark skinned from it, uninhabited, smooth as polished bone. The spring only revealed how dead it was, while pelting every other bush and tree with birds.

I sat and smiled to hear how loudly and persistently they shouted their pieces of language. It was a sunless afternoon, close and scented. The white butterfly, early hatched, was half blown, half lifted over the thick golden gorse. Two blackbirds were singing from opposite sides of the valley. 'Tee oh tee!' they sang, and waited, singing carelessly and listening intently as if only when it left their happy breasts had the song a value for them. Of all the birds I think they are the ones whose voices come nearest to our idea of music. In between the flourishes which pierce miles of distance, undulating with the hills, there are none of those strident intervals with which the thrushes contrast their purer notes. Perhaps the thrush is the greater musician. The blackbird is a wild boy while he sings, but having sung he seems to listen to his notes travelling over the earth with an intense and detached wonder expressed in his silent poise.

It made me smile, it made me laugh to hear those birds!

The thrush: 'All *right* then.' And passionately: 'I don't *believe* it.'

'Chee–chee–chee–chee–women's institute!' rattled a chaffinch. This is Sian's interpretation of his comical gush, and since she pointed it out, I have always thought it the most distinct articulation in bird sound.

'Tee oh tee!' repeated the blackbird buoyantly. Then all the little birds began whirring and chipping, and the cuckoo pendulum swung against the horizon wall. Finches and wrens and robins, pippets, linnets, yellowhammers were all grinding and sharpening their small notes, like a workshop, where harsh magpies swore and woodpeckers laughed madly against their own tapping.

'Cheat-cheat-cheat!' cried a little unseen voice. And I heard a little sturdy note clanging from the ivy-curtained undergrowth over and over again—the blacksmith bird. But above all the blackbird, the idle beauty, lost in singing and the for ever too late effort to regain what he had sung!

Then all went quiet except 'Cheat cheat,' and a bee. Nettles were growing through the grass, clouds made the green heavy. And I smelled the bluebells. It was then that I thought I should like to try and write something of this profound inner and outer life-awareness, of this deep exciting solitude, outwardly so quiet, but lived as a nun lives with her soul, as a lark with its song in the sky over an open field silver combed by air and light. A life full of fervent, ardent beauty whose meaning, like Wordsworth's meditation, lies between unknown words; whose senses, one and many, touch in earth all things. There are gods: but to them we can give only the same heart that we give to humanity. To nature, to earth, we can give our real inmost undistorted being. There are no wonders comparable to the wonders of the earth if it is loved. The cuckoo's voice changes the world. A yellow-flowering weed makes one a child again, and the grasses' touch in the evening is drink to the flesh. Something that is all of summer's open joy is visible in the white butterfly's shaggy flight. As he floats and sinks against the green shadows in the trees he seems a mote from the white clouds, coasting the outline of a cumulus filled with leaves . . .

Oh to be alone, to be alive! Solitude is marvellous to the body. To the inner soul which is united by a physical and spiritual affinity to the life in all things, its own innocent existence pledges joy.

Smelling the bluebells I thought I would try to write this for people who feel and understand these matters. For people who work in the fields and gardens and then go to bed in the twilight, aware of the stars. They have a nymph who lives in trees and seasons; and for them every flower and creature and sound in the sun's brood has its special invocation.

To me there is a peculiar familiar mood which comes when I hear bees and walk by great horse-chestnut trees in bloom, and see round my feet dandelions and buttercups. I could as easily explain my being alive as define what is that far-back association. When soft rain falls my nymph leaps. And when I see the chestnut blooms a peace that is older than myself, becomes me. Others love even the thought of tall cow parsley, green and white because in its season delight and pleasure come to meet them.

I did get out my pen. But just as I was beginning a cicada clicked in the grass and I went to look for it. From tussock to tussock I searched under the dead grass, but the clicking jumped ahead from insect to insect, until at last I stood on the top of the valley wall, with all the trees below me, and the daisies all around in the short grass, burst open in the heat.

On the hill ridge there was calm while down below the hollow streamed with sound and movement. So many tinges, so many greens, vague and sharp, blended down there that it was like a cloud filled with a rainbow. I sat down, and close by my foot a bee came and sat on a buttercup. The blackbird my side of the brook had flown farther off, his notes blown away from me by the wind which lifted the butterflies over the bracken paths I had left. In the sudden stillness where I sat the arrested sunbeams could be felt warming and drying the grass. Sweeping my hand over it I could feel a moist glow in the palm, a blood heat thrilling as the breath of a fountain. The stillness fell from between cloud and cloud and was timed in the per-petual blue spaces. I heard a lark's song, like a nucleus, very high and rarefied, swarming in the sky; and minute sounds broke off the hills—a lamb's bleat, the grunt of a wagon wheel rolling over stones miles away. Putting my face down I could hear an undertone of distance, distinct and dwindled . . . the wheat hissing round the edges of the fields, the sweet roar of pollen-seeking bees in the willows, even the minute crinkling noise the insects made creeping over grass blades.

And I could look down and see under me the form of the valley seen through leaves as a cloud is seen through rain. Nets of buds were thrown over the branches, where, among the rich, pallid flowers, bees made slow eddies of pollen and scent. In the green crack the wind waves were rolling out their deep song which nothing can detain on its way to the heart.

On the hills one can hear the clouds, their soft thunder slipping, their tenderness, the heat they pour down on the moist leaves. The sky becomes something the understanding can grasp. In the valley it is the impact—the brood within the nest. The smell of the flowers, the warmth and the rain drops drying, is almost within sight.

Sitting on the hilltop watching a bee clutch the bare stem of a buttercup I remembered how I love to walk along the stream knowing what it means to live alone with no imparted teaching. I accept only the light of my own understanding. I would rather that small glow-worm in my breast than to be or receive histories and prophecies. In my world the hills, the trees, and the fields fulfil every spiritual wish, every tangible form which my brain and body can imagine. Humanness tells me that one's death will be lonely. But then, to return to what inhabits and moves me . . . No matter how many people share the earth, solitude is invulnerable. In perception there is no collision. Having once entered it there can be no numbers.

This morning in the cottage doing my work, mentally I touched the wet flowers. The wood sorrel like a linnet's egg, its white petals incurving, traced with their lines of veining. The seeing blue of the speedwell's wet eye magnified by the round bead of rain in it. All the flower shapes—the white, the blue, the gold, I saw, I touched with my fingers, out in the rain under the trees, while the drops flowed over, leaf by leaf, descending green ladders to the earth.

BEET HOEING

BEFORE I set out this morning our small grey bees were on the wing. I went down to look at the hive to see if they seemed like swarming, but it was most peaceful work they had in mind. The whole width of the opening was full of their dusty little bodies which turned golden as they flew up into the sunlight. Some were already returning, crawling up the alighting board, their legs bowed in breeches of pollen. As they darted up and circled they became atoms of sun, separated and whirling in the atmosphere. The feeling of morning is inexpressible. The effervescent air is so light a leaf disturbs it; so true, so spiritually faithful to it is the response of the mood in me that I can think of no other time; and yet night clings, and its influence persists like an impression of a dream still damp on the brain.

I don't know what it is I want in the morning, unless it is everything—everything in the World and the Sky. Could I go in *all* directions my heart might be satisfied. I want the dew, the hills, the sky and the grass. I want the first movements of my body, the first steps to be the first and yet to go on for ever.

As I go to work the lark's song is in the clear sky and down in among the buttercups. How slowly, how exquisitely the drop of dew is gathered into the thinning air, the wrinkled cloud is solved! There is a strange *abstemiousness* in the way the bird sings, the pale sky drinks the earth. A faint silveriness tingles over the unformed blue of space, and an unmarred silence lies as yet behind the spacious sounds of wind and wakening.

I do believe that we are born of morning and not of flesh and blood . . .

It happened that during my first bout of hoeing we had a group of perfect days and nights. Not one here and another a week afterwards, but a lustrous sequence, shining like a constellation in the void of the year. It was then that I saw I really belonged to a world which belonged to the sun. The light lasted in the evening beyond the utter end, and beyond the uttermost moment, neither did the stars appear in the visible universe. The nights were only slender bridges of shadow, and the northern sky divided the two clear red lakes of dawn and sunset only by the subtler light of reflection.

There was calm in the sky, and a pause as it were, on earth after the first rapid unfolding of leaf, flower and field. Certain aspects of those days and nights I never shall forget—the mornings filled with dew and space and the light which transcended all detail; the transparent moon hanging edge to earth and the luminous green of Garway's bracken breaking through the mist: in the evenings hearing the partridges' call over the clover field when we were undressing for bed and the rasp of the cricket in the dusky garden under the window, the flight of the blonde moths round the flowers. I remember the cricket sounded like a tiny wrist watch being wound, and that the moths were white or brown specks according to whether they were seen against the hedge or the sky. And besides these things I never could forget the freedom of limbs and spirit, the ease and the joy. Those nights and days come back to me now: and the feelings I had are more real to me at this moment than the clouds, the rain, and the parting from M——.

I kept a small Nature diary of the eternal interest and entertainment in the fields, nor did I know where to stop or what to leave out. At night we used to bathe in a stream that flowed with fern shadow, and rinse away under a waterfall, the dust from the paths that were like hot pink bricks to walk on. It was a delight to lie on the bed, at length, covered only with the calm bright twilight.

At midday there came no sound or bustling from the wide open doors. The farms rested under their acres of roofs and the dogs slept. The channel of the paths wound deeply through the uncut hay: the branching buttercups reflected the sun in their petals. How softly the grass touched my legs as I walked to the field; how the woodpecker laughed, and the doves purred! How quiet and cooling the sight of the elms with their deep dark green holes of shade in them!

When I set off on that morning my feet were soaked in the dew before I reached the stream at the bottom of the hill. I saw the backs of the sheep feeding near by all as one level like the seemingly floating depth of the hay grass, or curving to the hill in a halo outside its own contour. While I stood there looking at the flowers a flock of young pullets came thudding down on the hard track for the scraps I'd put for them in my dinner basket, and while their yellow feet skidded and drummed on the grass and they were snatching the bits from under one another's beaks, I pulled a wild rhubarb leaf and looked at the summer clouds so silver bright between the stems of the Italian rye grass. Then I went on again up the steep rise, noticing the white clover and yolk-yellow ladies' slipper in bloom among the thinning edges of the hay, where it was half path, half crop.

As I went into the field by the gate under the holly tree I caught the sound of the men's hoes chipping dully against dry soil and stones, and there was a cluster of sun-burnt straw hats down under the slope tucked into the world of glossy leaves and nodding slowly along in the current of the hoeing.

Then I pulled my hoe out of the hedge and went to my own patch.

The sky, with us, took the place of time. Only the cuckoo occasionally took up the moments, and as idly let them drop into silence. All day the field remained the same, only a higher light played in the polished leaves, and a clearer heat struck down. Jackdaws flew over, and plovers and pigeons, and the ladybirds crawled on the broken pink earth. Up and down the drills, leaving single plants about eighteen inches apart, cutting out weeds, hoeing now to the right and now to the left of the body, to rest the screwed waist. We hoed a hundred yards down the field and that was a 'brent'; a hundred yards up and that was another brent. Two brents make a 'bout,' and that is the whole language of hoeing.

It was a clean field with fine sappy leaved plants. The weeds were mostly pimpernel, a thistle now and then, a few plantains and two species of which I know only their country names, 'Fat Hen' and 'Dodder.' Fat hen is a tall slender plant with thin greyish-green leaves and grey sorrel-like flowers, but dodder made me think of pine needles with its long sharp bodkins of vivid emerald colour.

On the opposite hillside by an orchard stood a farm house and buildings, like a village in a field. The doors stood open and the smokeless chimneys cast their bent shadows over the roof. Paths went out from it across the fields, but no one walked along them, no one was ever seen looking out of its windows or moving in its yard or garden of burned grass. No one, no one all day. Neither steps, nor voices, nor barking dogs. The cattle and sheep about it grazed without sound, and its patches of shadow never seemed to change!

I used to look at it and wonder . . .

But one hot afternoon about four o'clock when the doves were blessing themselves over, and the small breeze was like a trickle of water in a wide and faded river bed, there came from that farm a terrible burst of childish sobbing and crying— a tumultuous sound so wild and brief that it seemed instantaneous. And that was the sole manifestation of any sort of life that took place in a month. Once I spoke about the strange silence and stillness over there, and a man told me he didn't know why it should be, but it was always the same.

I was perfectly happy hoeing alone and thinking, feeling the sun burning my arm above the elbow where it jutted into the light, feeling rather than *seeing* the birds that bent over my head and into the trees, listening to the laughing and the talking of the men in the far corner without gathering one separate word.

But much as I liked the work, what I loved was the dinner hour, when sitting under the hedge I could think about what I saw. During the actual work my body seemed to lull its own senses and to call upon only those parts which it needed.

I used to feel that in some profound way, my body was becoming my soul.

If you go in for the leisurely and meditative work of the fields (meditative in the deep physical sense) or if you are merely in the habit of walking slowly and often and happily in among the grass and the trees and the streams, you feel this oneness perpetually. To me hoeing brought no monotony but rather peace and fulfilment as though the eternal longing of the body for justification before the spirit was being accomplished in an action which nature in me made natural to the world. It was when I thought of the work *before me*, I felt its monotony. There *was* monotony and to some quick brains there would be an intolerable levelling of thought; or, sharper to bear, a constant staring at the unchanged images aspected in the mind. Every one of us has a shadow or a light within him, too sombre or too keen for constant scrutiny, and solitary, blunt, repetitive action is no defence against too good or too bad an idea. Listless outward senses which cannot distract, labour which is habitual, unhazardous, hard and slow in its effect upon a landscape, leaves a man too close to his own pain or delight. If I could form a choral it would be to loneliness, that a thousand voices should praise one voice: but I can imagine a solitude which is agony, when a man and himself are *apart* and gazing unremittingly at each other. That is why I think that in slow handwork out of doors, work without machinery to rouse the competitive brain, any soothing pleasure, like smoking and talking, should be encouraged. Anything that intervenes, that shields and mitigates. The work many are doing to-day is never original or fresh—is in a sense worn out, and was habit a thousand years before it became habit to those who are doing it now.

But, like Thoreau sitting in his doorway watching the summer rain, I smiled incessantly at my good fortune. I like to be alone with all the strength I can muster—at least when I am in the fields. For myself I would rather not talk at all, and rather not listen too much to others. I think in a language I cannot speak, and the sounds I hear often speak to my thoughts in the same untranslatable idiom. Being slower than the men it was necessary that I should hoe alone, or else they would be always passing me; then either I had to stop, or they had to stop or we all clashed and entangled our hoes, trampling the beet, and hardening the ground. Not only that: my pay was 10*d.* an hour and so I felt that my pace didn't justify my frequent standing aside if it could be helped.

So I hoed alone and was happy alone. I like to tend what is going to be eaten, and I like to feel that I'm getting nourishment out of my food even before it is ripe in the ground. A diet of sugar beet at the end of a five-foot hoe is not likely to be recommended by any except those who recognize that some foods should never reach the mouth. But it suited me. There is a fragrance in fresh, broken soil, an exhalation like *rising* rain. And a companionship transcending the human scope of sympathy is to be experienced in the fields out under the clouds, in the sun's touch and the wind's presence ever beside you. I was happy at work, happiest at noon resting and seeing. The farmer paid me wages: it was money with the sun on it, money which I needed. But the trees held out more to me with their green branches. I received that which no farmer could pay or grudge me getting, from the great flat ivory elder blossoms—all that richness and delicacy was mine though I never touched one. Every moment the universal year was telling me the visible version of Time in the hedge blooms, in the first wheat ears, in buttercups, and clover and wild honeysuckle.

So, in the foreshortened noon, when the earth seemed lowest, the hot sky emptiest of flight, I sat in the hedge and watched a world which was as though held still in a power greater than itself. About four o'clock my back would be aching, but at dinner time I was not much tired, though my legs and arms seemed bewildered by the sudden cessation of a pattern and rhythm which had held them enthralled. My body was still away in a harmony of movement which somehow translated into occupation the flowing of the sky, the continuousness of the earth . . .

Sitting in the hedge I would hear the sticks and twigs crackle behind my shoulders and the docks and nettles brushed my neck with their cool and peppery touches. With a great leaf on my head I would stretch out my legs beyond the dwindling shadow of a hawthorn, into the sunlit straw-strewn track, and feel the dusty burning of my feet inside my sandals. Often, during those first intensely hot days, sweat would break out on my face and breast as I leaned back after my dinner looking either at the listless field, or at the wrinkled green scum on the pond by the elder tree. Sometimes with a faint tearing noise the coarse grass and reeds would part and a moorhen would paddle away from me out into the middle of the pond, at the point of a 'V' of light. Sometimes a sparrow would alight on the faded muck heap, and with his tail perked up, would cast me a quick, miserly glance. I often wondered that I never saw a snake come to bask. The hot heaps of dirt and muck, weeds and straw, which lay by the path would have been the ideal depository for their eggs.

But no sound of bird or beast, no flight, no leafy whisper, no white 'V' upon the pond, ever filled out the space either of thought or of fact. As small, as powerless as the men's voices and the shallow tinkling of their hoes, to fill the width and weight of the sky, was the flight of a jackdaw, the cuckoo's cry, the bleating of the weary sheep and cattle spreading slowly over the green hills. The silence was the day itself, the thought itself: and life used it as a covering, as an artifice to conceal its own necessary restlessness. I don't know why, but at the middle hour when the heat seems as if it can neither fall nor rise, all natural life seems to show itself only under disguise. The birds are at their shyest, and dive and soar as if they would pass not only through but *behind* the sunlight: the butterflies weave columns of flight about one another as though each insect were trying to screen itself behind the wings of its fellow: and so perpetually they climb into the silvery blue higher and higher until the light dissolves the competition: the flies and beetles dart like thieves, the birds delude you with a leaf, the spiders with the dust. Behind the stalks, in the narrow shadows which separate the grasses, eyes are watching, nerves are waiting for the order and peremptory opportunity to move and leap. The apparent twiddling of an ox-eye daisy is not only a tiny whirlwind but a big beetle running up the stem to hide under the flower. And there he clings tight with the petals spread over him, looking up as I look up into the hawthorn, wondering and meditating, until instinct makes him run down again as fast.

I look up full of wordless wonder, and down, nor do I know what thoughts are shaping in me, only that there is a boundless awareness which is ready to be anything it perceives from light itself, diffuse, impalpable, to the ants see-sawing over the grass blades. I see and contain the muscular growth of the hawthorn and the descent of a plover darting earthwards as if he meant to stab the point of his wing into the ground. Over the middle of the field, high and trembling, a hawk hovers, ethereal as a moth in the twilight and then suddenly he is gone as if the eye were blind to him. Speed is used by the wild creatures *not* for its own sake, but for concealment. There are flights which you cannot see, let alone what made them, for they are to you no more than instantaneous flashes and weals along the air. Leaves rustle without wind and shadows sometimes move queerly, ahead of the sun; it is all delusion. Sitting by the hedge I am in a world of counterfeit which I sense but cannot catch. My thoughts will only include the stillness, the sun, the midday of the pallid throbbing hills. Soon there will be the feel of the bright iron under a root, and the earth working into my shoes and pressing into my feet; and then again the evening, the clear sky, the garden and the dusty step. That is the essence of these days—that is their true length—the length the mind may travel to the dusk. It must come, the end which is so near the dawn, the twilight which is the sunrise. I long without wishing to hurry through the present, for the evening which I shall surely have, for the peace, and the sea-like calm upon the grass and the sky.

LITTLE NATURE DIARY

April 30th. This evening Gordon and Mr. Davis of Hoarwithy brought the bees and the hive was set up at the bottom of the garden.

The bees and the hive cost £5. We are buying another second-hand hive from Mr. Davis. He is painting it and letting us have it for £1. We shall try for a swarm.

He left his old coat in the kitchen.

M—— found a mouse in the chest. He took it in his hand—it was sleek and fat—but it slipped down his arm as if greased and ran under the cupboard.

May 1st. May Day. Last night I couldn't sleep for joy over the bees. The moon strewed the bed with leafy shapes and lines from the window. The night intensely still.

This morning I've been down by the hive getting them used to the sight of me. Sat on the path. Ate a piece of bread and cheese and looked at the strawberry flowers. As the sun grew hot the bees began to fly and hum about the garden. We put a saucer of water for them among the strawberry leaves with match sticks floating—this is until they find the stream.

It's a beautiful clear, windless day, all growing things still in the sunlight.

Later. The smell of watering . . . a low red magnified moon hanging in the mist along the field. The moonlight and the twilight. Going to bed without lamps or candles. The peculiar happiness of *seeing* it all so late—trees, wall, paths, flowers in their dark, wet patches.

May 2nd. Sitting in the sun in the upstairs window hearing a thrush and a lark. The dandelion clump in the wall—its flowers half shut. And the breeze stirring a dock leaf.

Oh the waking! When the field is grey with dew and clear

narrow smoke is rising from each cottage. The first yellow sunbeams flow . . .

May 3rd. Sunday. I am lying under the south bank with the direct sun in the pure blue sky shining into my ear and the corner of my eye. The flies are buzzing; the bramble has new, ribbed leaves, and a bee shuttles to and fro in the mouth of a rabbit hole. It must be a cast-off dwelling for there's a spider's web across the tunnel and grey lichen on the walls.

I have had my feet in the stream, and now the soles are burning. I can write no more. I have been lying here waiting for M—— to come down the hill from the farm. I, with every other thing; I am too alive to think of any particle of life. I am whole with the budding black knotted 'knights' whose stems are lengthening among the daisies. The butterflies, the trees and the sky . . .

May 4th. Rode Maggie Mare to Dingestowe. The Blue Door—no blue door. Felt the lovely heat of the sun on my thigh through the serge where my trousers were pulled tight. The saddle squeaking. The stonebreakers told me the way. The gypsy calling out of Monmouth market: 'Is she for sale? Stop, my pretty girl, where are you going? Stop just a minute.'

I shan't forget the far walls shining from the hazy hills, the farms faintly gleaming, the indistinct horizon. Llangrove's bare height, the field of kale stumps bitten clean, the jays. The little narrow stream flowing white between its turf banks, the shade and simple open hills. Passed a cottage with two beehives by the door—one made of old tins.

May 5th. This evening we put in the field potatoes. M—— planted them along the furrow and I followed hoeing them over. The row was two hundred and forty yards long, right across the bottom half of the field which was wheat last year. I had to keep stopping to rest. My left elbow was numb.

It's strange to be out in the middle of a field, alone, working till the sweat runs off you, for what object you can hardly tell. M—— was too far ahead to hear me: there was only the sunlight, the grooves the hoe made in the dry rattling soil, and the

146

solid body of the wind pressing always against my left side. White mare's tails were streaked across the sky: the sunlight was yellow and thin, the shadows on the green meadows long and pointed. When I began the row I dabbed at, and broke the clods, and tried to fine them as well as I could, jerking and *out of scheme*, and stopping all the time to look at what I'd done. But soon my action began to adapt itself to the size of the job and I worked as if it *were* a field and not a garden. My thoughts left me. The soles of my feet got sore and I seemed to be treading on hot sandpaper. I can see those hoe-marks . . . our row and the others looked as if they had been done by a machine, so regular were the shadows in the stroke. Sometimes a stone chinked against the hoe or a hairpin fell out of my hair. Coming home I heard the dove . . . the sky was primrose yellow, the first hint of twilight in the shadows. During the last week the level of the earth has floated higher on a flood of green. You can plunge your arm up to the shoulder in the flowers growing on the hedge banks. Up and up floods the year with all the blossoms on its surface ruffling, with the depth under, the buoyancy above . . . and then the small, separate, shaded clouds. . . .

Early morning. Watering the garden and boiling the kettle for my tea. The green sunlight over the hedge, the hills—oh the hills! Do I think, do I live, what is *my* nature, if ever it could be imagined apart? I seem to *be* in the light that pours down, that fills the sky. The smoke of the fire blows over the wall, and the money tree trembles as the grey film rushes upward. All the currant bushes are in motion, the butterflies in flight. It is happy and warm close under the bank where the dandelions flower.

> Perched on the wood pile, sparrow,
> sparrow what meaneth thy song
> with thy cool water-ball eye
> watching the swifts along?

Afternoon. I had to fetch water from the stream. As I went through the gate and over the grass silently swinging the bucket and can, there fell a sudden spell of still heat. The sheep were feeding on the slope: the shadows of the willows were flung wide from the dry bank to the stream over a half acre of dark green grass. Day by day now, the shadows rise. There is nothing out of doors that doesn't bring joy. Feeling the handles swinging I stepped down on the moving stone in the middle of the stream. Two chaffinches were there perched on the upturned slabs, their tails going up and down as they balanced and looked at one another and at me. Presently a third flew down, and then after circling and returning all three to rock themselves once more, they all flew up into the sunny willow.

A multiplicity of notes came down the stream. . . . After I'd rinsed and filled the buckets and set them on the grass, I sat down on the flat stone sheltered from the north by the sharp drop of the bank. I saw the grass growing up from the roots along the top of it, and the long locks of the violet plant dipping into the water. The willow leaves were still in light and shadow, the green about cooled the eyeballs. Two bees were humming a duet, turn and turn, the bumble bee with her sultry contralto sound, then the honey bee, clear and shrill, starting up again after a pause.

I washed my hands and held them in the water, gazing at the grain of the skin. And then some echo of another time made me look and remember. There is a land drain falls into the stream close by where I was sitting. Out of it, through its open mouth, trickles the clearest, most sparkling rill of water that ever nourished ferns and moist grass. To one side, on the slope is a small, vivid, emerald patch of sward, no larger than a man's dinner handkerchief. On this tiny lawn, one day I had seen a stoat playing by itself. It wasn't this time of year—indeed I've forgotten when it was, only that it was warm and still and my presence passed unsensed by the lovely creature whose solitary and most exquisite reiteration of subtlety and grace I shall always recall as one of the most entrancing things ever seen—a sight which will not only *characterize* the place to me forever, but in a sense *spiritualize* it. I have seen stoats playing before

(I saw a pair when I was very young) and found their movements even more beautiful than the happy adder's, as he turns to and fro in the sun. But this one! turning and winding, as if with an invisible companion to his joyous pattern of flow and bend, keeping always within the boundaries set by the little patch of green, best grass, how softly and silently his feet fell! As silently as the sunlight descends on the ground his four pads touched it. Like a shadow, a rift, a spirit creature without colour or sound. He must have been brownish or silvery red, but I didn't notice. All I seemed to see was silence, innocence, delight: silence in contrast with movement, and movement against still ground. I never pass the spot without the feeling of incompleteness that he isn't still there. If one must cease, rather he should be dancing alone, and the place have vanished. It has formed an ideal in me, a memory so perfect that I can hardly believe that the real thing ever happened. Only the green grass tells me, the willow branches, the water, and the gleanings of sunshine, that felt the stoat's solitude.

May 8th. A bitterly cold morning. The baker got me out of bed because it was Good Friday and he wanted to get his round over. Only the lark seemed happy (she brushes an earwig off the paper with grimy fingers, only the lark, she thinks). The grey clouds and faint blue pleased him, and the light of fields and trees. In the garden I could see my reckless breath blowing away on the north wind as in December.

Afterwards I sat sewing. The cottage was so quiet that I realized how it must be when I'm not in it. The clock ticked in the back kitchen, the fire settled, the sun shone through the windows. And there were sounds in the furniture, among the population, like a person curling into an armchair with a deep sigh of peace. Even the kettles and saucepans boiled with only the softest of bubblings. . . .

I realized how tired my body was, and wondered if it's often so, and can't tell me because I won't heed. I sat in the big chair darning socks and smoking. Bang! in walked the man with the frames and foundation for the second hive. And instantly *I lost ear*.

Walked over to Patty's and lay on the grass talking to her and to her mother. Patty's skin is turning brown. She sits in her invalid chair, looking at the trees. A tom-tit lives in the great oak before the cottage. They say it sings all day. Strange—the huge tree and the tiny bird, the tiny splash of song!

Mrs. Josephs sat on a tree stump, her chin on her fists. Her eyes seem to grow a deeper colour with looking. When she just glances they are just grey, but when they rest on the sky or the grass they gather a deep *seeing* blue. She looks at a thing as if she saw its past in it. The park . . . the water . . .

Oh Lord, this week I have done so much. The potatoes, the double wash, the ride to Dingestowe. Now the hive. Oh Lord, let thy servant put her hand in the stream.

May 9th. Sunday. It was very cold. The clouds blowing and closing up. No sun. The tulips shut. The earth dark and green. When we started out clusters of raindrops hit us in the face. Fetched the hive. All the frames and the inside of the roof, all the cracks full of black veil-like eggs and white nymph cases. We trundled it along in the barrow. Tea at Panbrook. There was something delicious in the flavour of the room, in the wood fire, the rain falling, the lilac. The doorstone was wet. Looked at old books and prints.

Evening. Supper by the fire. It was a very dark, starless night with the rocking of our lilac tree, and a great void at the window.

May 10th. Oh so lovely! to go out and see the black earth round all the little seedlings, all washed and refreshed. The birds were singing, the thrush inhaling his notes when I awoke.

The bees are still springcleaning and carrying out those which died on the journey. About a dozen dead are lying under the alighting board, on their backs, with stiff wings half open. It's pathetic and queer to observe how complete is death, how detailed, that it can make *rigor* of a bee, a leaf, a tiny, tiny red beetle, which possibly only one other creature in the universe, knew and felt existed.

May 11th. Dark, cold, lowering.

May 12th. The fourth cold, cloudy morning. The earth is darkened by the clouds of its own green. Yet there is something wonderfully gentle and hopeful in the air. Through every open window and door I hear birds singing, courage.

Last night when I was lying awake with my eyes closed I saw flowers. I saw the dead nettle—every vein, every leaf, and the stalk and the bloom. And the speedwell, closed as in rain, with the silver-blue petals furled . . . and the green dots of the wild parsley in bud.

Later. Thomas Catto *woven* into the wood pile. The weather changed: the sun came out. Great blue and lurid clouds thickened the hot air. All the bees crowded on and around the alighting board—dancing and whirling in the air before the hive, it seemed either in mad ecstasy or wild and migratory mood. I was afraid of a swarm and worked in the garden to watch them.

The evening was the light, the eye of the day. A serene dusk closed round the red sun. The golden level on the tree trunks, moving up the stems of the keck, pointing the grass tips.

We walked by the brook and down the meadows. The day-old foal was running beside her dappled mother. With a silky swish their hooves went through the grass . . . the only sound. Then under the apple tree they stopped, and the mother nosed her baby, bending her bright neck. A glimpse of the sheep feeding on the hill, dark grey, with luminous backs. One lamb was at the gate looking through into the lane. From this spot we heard the stream; but the most minute and distinct sound was a wild bee booming in the bank of the lane. That's the essence of such an evening—a late bee working among swinging leaves, and the dew appearing.

May 13th. There's one beautiful bird . . . The cottage is filled with the contrast of red sunlight and deep shadow. The sunlight falls on the stairs, is ingrained in the furniture. The blackbird's 'Tee-tee-tee'—and the chaffinch. A spider running across the path, like a bead rolling.

I went to Ross and lugged out with me a dozen young stock plants and waterproof felting for the hive. M—— finished painting the second, and we looked inside our own. The cells not capped.

I gardened. Now it's all over for to-day except a bit of ironing. Tammas Cat is sitting on the windowsill of our bedroom sniffing the smell of digging. I sit with my arms on the table looking out. Bees in the lilac: the sun right ahead over Garway, which is so grey and tender a tone, yet a strong line. Stiller even than the calm of sky and earth is my thought. I can see the thistle balls shining in the clover, and the grey, orange and violet clouds gleaming in a sort of haze. It's lovely. Utterly beautiful. I am in the middle of loveliness, and peace.

May 14th. . . . As I went along I felt a few raindrops. The sky was a light piercing grey—not a wet grey but a silvery tingling shadow, as at morning before sunrise.

Later. The sun long gone in, the south wind blowing tenderly, smelling of bluebells and gorse. The midges whirling over the stream between the tree boles. Walking with my head down I saw the bumble bee, very black and large against the pearly grass, sipping from some tiny yellow flowers. There's a bird I shall call the ivy bird, or simply the shade bird. 'Tching-tchang, tching-tchang,' are his two notes, and whenever I hear them they come from some dark little spinney or old dying hedgerow which is all matted with the dark shade of ivy and elder and holly. Must find out what he is. Such a sunless song, sharp, cold, expressionless like a little chip of steel between hammer and anvil. Yet a very solitary sound—one that you don't hear unless you are alone and moving quietly. Another bird was singing 'I don't believe it,' over and over again. The path was baked a light pink; the wych elm a whitey-green, shedding its flowers. I had taken a linen sheet to patch but had no sooner settled on the grass by the stream than I had to run back home again and take the clothes off the line. The rain prickled . . . Polly and her foal in the orchard. The foal was lying on its side by a fallen apple trunk, in a deaf sleep. It was so thin it looked flat, as if cut out. Suddenly it got on its legs, wagged its ears and began to suck. It has a very soft, dull black coat with a lighter bloom, like soot. Standing and looking at it from behind it seems to be only a narrow spine, a pair of enormous ears, in shape resembling laurel leaves, and four long legs which look as if they had been driven so far up into its body that they are coming through.

I picked flowers to paint . . . here is sunlight making the hedges yellow against the grey sky. I was going to have a fire by the stream and sit and sew and listen to the water.

May 15th. In the early morning planted out a few lettuces in my dressing gown. Had a fire outside by the woodpile and boiled a sheep's head on it. I wondered how the research worker reacts, and how the human dissector, when, after we had eaten our dinner, I found in a crevice of the sheep's skull the loathsome, flat, flabby maggot which causes gid. There were two of them, in the sinus cavity, boiled, full of what had been the animal's brain tissue. The fly or insect which causes gid is breathed up from the ground through a sheep's nostrils when it is cropping the field. Perhaps it's the egg, or embryo—I'm not sure. But one sheep with the gid infects the ground with it. Once breathed, it lodges in the frontal cavity and there develops into a large maggot. Then it works or is worked round to the base of the skull, whence it reaches and touches the brain proper. The sheep then begins to show it has the gid, and goes round and round until it is killed. I've seen one. I asked Mr. Josephs whether one couldn't drill the bone and extract the maggot, to save life. 'Yes, if you knew where it was. But you can't tell. Besides, until the sheep began to go giddy you wouldn't know it was there at all.'

In the afternoon I went to see Patty. A strong wind blew and the sun shone hot on my back as I crossed the big meadow. Noticed the flat plantains and the wide dry yellow grasses under the hedge, like satin ribbon. The stitchwort and the speedwell and the grass glittering with buttercups and daisies, all out since I went this way last week. . . . I could see the Josephs' great oak tree smiling in the sun and Patty sitting under it. The two little girls came along the green path through the middle of the flowery field, in pink and jade green dresses. The elder carried a bunch of purple iris and blue bell flowers. They were going into the graveyard. As I stepped forward the sun and the flowers made me so happy that I could have stopped at every stride. . . . Mrs. Josephs was leaning up to the hedge with arms outstretched feeling for a bird's nest. There's no other family in this district which is so aware of the life around them—the plants, the secret play places and the habits of animals. They can tell where the chaffinch has built, how the blackbird is rearing a second brood and where in the solitary underwood the sparrow is stripping the flowers and green fruit from the wild currant bush. Mrs. Josephs turned round, smiled, fixed a hairpin, and sat down on a log. Her eyes were so clear a blue that looking into them I felt I was seeing through her head into the sky behind. Almost the first remark she made was: 'Aren't the buttercups beautiful? They've come so suddenly. Oh I do think the field's lovely now!' Her little chicks were cheeping in the grass under the tree and Toby the sheepdog was chasing bees. The whole countryside shone around us, clouds and trees, hills and green meadows. But sitting there the wind was a perpetual shadow in the sunlight.

Later. The sun is out of sight, shining from a hidden infinity, into one line of light farther than all the rest of the sky. The clouds look like land—the clover and the corn a dark, thick green.

Margaret has one old cider apple tree whose blossoms are a dead chalky white. The chestnut flowers white and candy pink, falling by the roadside.

May 19th. Washed, gardened. M—— has been in bed with a chill this last two days. A long windy day; then calm. I didn't finish the hoeing until the late, last sunset was red beyond the darkened hills and torpid trees . . . the clouds seemed separating themselves from the moon until she shone alone in a calm soft blue between the oak tree and a star. . . . I came in and stood by the kitchen window watching the clearness and the darkness. On the wall a faint ladder of moonlight and shadow.

May 20th. The wild parsley on either side of me, the hills and low sky stained with dark storm blue—a great wash or blend of colours which seemed running over and down the bare line of the horizon.

I slept in the front room. Half woke very early and knew it was the sun rising which scattered the red fleece over the walls and ceiling. The mirror, the furniture, the field, were seen by me through a flamy haze while the dream landscape thawed within my brain . . . the clouds upon the sky were as though ingrained, like the first red ripeness streaking an apple.

When I jumped out of bed and looked down on the flowers, I saw our tame blackbird, alert and trim, gathering stuff for her nest—her second. She filled her beak with bits of dead grass, weed and pale stalks which had blown over the wall. When she had collected quite a faggot she departed, and I got dressed. I couldn't help thinking that she looked just as if she were going home to boil a kettle. Digging along the hedge I turned up a large, jointed chrysalis about as big as a dry runner bean with a long sharp tail-piece which it wriggled, plate over plate. It was a bright mahogany red, like an unripe black cherry. And one rather cold gloomy afternoon I saw the worms coupling in the wet earth, bent like hoops, with their heads and tails buried.

Somebody asked Mr. Saunders if he wasn't afraid to work in his garden so near our bees: 'No, their path do go the other way,' he said. I never knew of the bees' pathway before but every one affirms its existence, and that all bees make and keep to one. Ours fly west, down to the stream. When the sun gets hot one can see the flow of them over the green clover, over the hump of hill, down to the valley where they bend the bluebells down. For us, to walk along the stream is to hear our bees working, and then we feel like farmers strolling through their cattle and flocks.

May 21st. In the evening it grew still sultrier. The yellow-green sunlit trees shone *at* the grey sky and the raindrops fell as if numbered. The earth and fields and hedges were bright: where the white clouds rolled over them the low larks sang, the thunder shifted. The stunted dandelions by the gate opened flat on the ground; the buttercups unfurled and one hoarse plover tossed himself up and down and cried above the roof.

I was searching for flat stones for my edging in the heap of builders' refuse thrown up against our garden wall. Gladys was wading deep into the clover. All was vivid and separately interesting to me—the coarse round stemmed grasses growing in tufts out of the red, sandy heap; my shadow, creased by the wall; the flat grey stones and porridgy lumps of rough casting hidden in nettle and dock and mallow plants. I saw the glimmer of dandelion balls far out in the green, and the whitey specks of moths ceaselessly flying over the hedge, dissolving from sight as soon as they came against the sky.

I picked up a fairly large stone which had pressed its shape into the sodden ground. It was part of the roof of an ants' nest; for, as I turned it over, there were the infinite people in infinite turmoil, jostling and running around one another in the first eager stampede to haul away and hide the precious eggs and nymphs. For several seconds all was mingle-mangle. Terror, trifling and trivial, worked upon the host like a draught upon sparks blowing them together and apart, driving them now to rush over and cling to the uprooted stone, now to set all upon and seize one egg while dozens lay defenceless. But *not one* ant tried to escape alone, to save her own life. Of that I am sure. Not a single ant retreated without a load into the caves which abounded in the porous cliffs. What is more, though this is uncertain, I believe that, a journey made, they returned once more to help clear the space where their naked treasures lay, so white, so terribly conspicuous, scattered openly, under the preying sky. I thought I would watch. So I sat down and leant over them. The panic passed soon; and with the utmost deftness, gallantry and resource each ant took a cocoon by the head and began dragging it uphill, and sometimes up precipices, to safety and shelter.

I'll tell it at leisure and in detail, for it was very wonderful. They were a dark, very dark brown race, and their nymphs showed up among them like grains of rice, half as long again as themselves. Proportionately they were as double-bed bolsters to smallish-sized landladies. There was something in the grip too which recalled the business of bed-making. . . .

By their own strength the ants transported every one up the porous, precipitous, utterly fantastic mountain side of grass roots and broken bricks. Engrossed to the point of suspended breathing, yet deeply moved, I stayed by them utterly unheeded. They seemed as if they knew that there was danger over them, but did not think of me any more than of my shadow. Since their code seems to forbid cowardice, or their behaviour to reject it, little can it matter to them by what they are attacked. Their one course they take; and their one form of fear, anxiety for their visible unborn, becomes protective before it can be isolated. It is almost tangible, this devotion, which the one common impulse expresses—almost it intervenes and interferes with one's observation. In three minutes the space was clear and the last 'bolster' could just be seen turning a sharp angle.

I had seen how two ants would help each other to get the burden into the easiest position, then one alone would half drag, half carry it away while the other (who seemed to belong to a band of those whose business it was to lift rather than to shift) would hurry on to the next one who needed her. I had seen how with inexorable self-control they laboured, refusing, if they knew where it hung, clouding them, to regard my presence. Now I was to see a problem for thought, not habit: and though they could not solve it neither would they leave it. Two cocoons and a half-dozen or so ants had been marooned on the stone, and the cocoons had rolled down into a v-shaped crevice from which it seemed they couldn't be extracted, or, having been, be lowered safely to the ground—a drop of about a hundred feet to them, with the stone curving into a smaller base than the surface on which they were imprisoned. Never did creatures show greater distress. They ran to the edge and signalled—none could reach them, and none could they reach. How they tried! At last with a fine grass stem I gently flicked the cocoons out of the crack and on to the ground. Instantly the marooned ants proved that alone and unladen they *could* have escaped, for somehow they lowered themselves, and in a minute, the cocoons were hurried out of my sight.

Later. How pleasant it was in the field! Growing was the earth's occupation . . . how shall I say it?—the trees and the flowering weeds, miles and miles of them in the grass—they bloomed as though by *inspiration* now that the wrestling at the root was over.

24. *Sunday*. I saw the green woodpecker. He screamed, and billowed over the stream in one leap, where we cross on the stones.

Bluebells, May, in flower. The rain in mist about the trees. The brook pool, black, green and gilded like a starling's breast . . . and the raindrop circles throbbing . . .

25. Trees clashing in wind and rain. In the evening sunlight pointing over the field. But all the buttercups folded, and the slim grass heads grey and bending.

26. *Early morning*. Saffron sky, grey field. The morning was coloured like a bird! Hanging on a branch of cloud—the sun, fruit of an oak.

Evening. Upstairs by the front window. Catty lying along the windowsill, his paws on an open book. The wych elm flowers drooping sideways, out of the green pottery jar. Rooks, cuckoos, thrushes, now the tom-tit. The cuckoo's call lies on the sky like a reflection on water. Sunlight after heavy rain. The sky is very pure light blue, and I see the moon half through it. I can't sit downstairs. The fire kills me. I remember Davis' poem. Up here I see. As I see more I hear more—the wind, the churr of small birds.

At the sink I saw still light lying on and between the hills. Then came the rain on all the green—heavy, loud, windless.

It took possession of the earth. There was no other life, no other sound.

> The poet felt the rain
> falling on his hair
> like a dreamer's light
> given everywhere;
>
> Given from the cloud,
> given from the moon,
> from the shells of spheres
> hidden in the noon.
>
> Underneath a leaf
> a silent bird, aloof,
> listened to the rain
> on his trembling roof.

Just after it stopped one silvery lark began to sing.

In the later evening I took Gladys out. The rooks flew off their nests and circled warily round the elm tops. The yellow and green fields showed as low bars between the trunks. They were rich with sunlight. At the cottages tin baths put out under spoutings—the road drying, dull and brilliant. A wonderful song from a thrush hidden in an oak tree . . . solitary, unmatchable notes, clear as a bugle. Voices in the uphill gardens flung up behind walls. Through an open door on to the road I saw into a tiny room where an old man was sitting at a table with his shirt sleeves wrinkled up his arms. He wore a black patch over his eye.

I stopped at a gate into a wheatfield. All was quiet on that hilltop except for a cuckoo which was cracking on its last syllable. A little way into the corn was a patch of broad, dark, glossy blades, like a spot of permanent shadow on the field. The sun had gone in: the sky was troubled with swift blue and grey. The edges of the trees moved ceaselessly.

28. . . . now I hear a light footstep going round the cottage.

I won't look. . . . I went to Ross. The market-place smelt of tomato plants set out in thousands beside the steps. Everybody was buying them, carrying them in their arms. Last night a strange, impulsive dream. A youthful procession dancing along, by trees, over an horizon, all dressed in white and gold. Once I had danced there with them. Two girls I had known came springing hand in hand over the grass. They were like narcissi.

29. Deep thought is still. It enters as itself, as a thing seen to the soul, as the wonderful colour of the speedwell's eye which looks at you, and seems to say, 'I am pure, pure.' Through and through it is itself.

The land is beyond imagery this wild weather. Solemn the hills with the flashing of wet grass-heads, the opening of the wind and the light; armed go the skylines.

I have done no housework this morning but sit writing at the upstairs window. Between the trees, where the green meadows shine, a bay horse is feeding. The grass bows to the east: the sky is full of splendour. Among the clover is a patch of yellow flowers. The grass there is tinged with heather colour; and there grows in it a great burdock plant and docks with leaves all broadly shaded. Beyond the buttercups a man mends his garden fence.

I sit thinking with the sky, and the charlock flowers and the bird notes.

30. Did the bees. We saw two emerging from transformation sleep, and a pair sparring on the roof of the hive.

Coming home along the lane, just at the noose of the two hills where the valley knots the brook, looking along the ground, I saw a marvellous and beautiful cloud, rising up from the grass like a white flame. Behind it the sky was solid storm, and before was spread the plain green hillside, heavy with sunlessness. All, all seemed breathless—willows, cloud and space. Suddenly a little bird like a lark darted in front of me and hovered over the road. Its wings whirled about it—it trembled and whisked the air round its body into a silver ball—as though it were enclosed in a crystal.

In the evening with M—— to Patty's, carrying the broken

umbrella, flapping like a damaged rook. We sheltered in the niches of a big oak, and watched the long rain shooting into the meadow grass. The birds at Langstone singing with such joy! The oxe-eyes are out and taller than the wheat, the hawthorns blooming in the melancholy green. We walked through the sheep . . . some shorn and in midsummer whiteness.

31. Handley took me to see a young owl in its nest. It was in a cracked pear tree on the ground. Nettles waved round the hole. We thrust our faces close and thought we could see a greyish spot which might have been the twilight of that hollow place gleaming on its down. But our heads were between the hole and the sun.

Last night the moon shone wide and wide over the separate clouds. White, compact, upon the blue, they showed to me the deep, delighted stars! It seemed as though I saw them suddenly! and then something started out of my breast, as though rushing to a meeting! The moon was out of sight behind the roof so that her light for me was without a centre, a source of vision by which to search for other lights. But the stars were rounds of self-contained light, pure at the centre, pure throughout. Almost I could distinguish their individual shapes—some long and dropping, like pendants shining with a calm intensity which went through me; others diamonded, with many facets whose restlessness hindered them. But all seemed my natural companions, sympathizing through *their* state of being, with my own. And with one another's. I saw that they seemed to *know* their relationships. So much they knew, that they had chosen to shape the blanks of space into the imaginary lines of constellations, as sound holds silence in shape as I myself, and the world and the earth are held in shining light and shining song. I leant against the porch and thought as I listened to the grass, what if a great planet fell, even if earth were untouched? Wouldn't it be as a rivet falling out of the universe, as molten silence pouring through torn sound? Shouldn't we all, even to our hearts and physical beings, collapse and die from universal haemorrhage? Sympathy shapes all.

Later. M——'s mother came. We went with them to show them another way home. Walked from St. Omens Cross. A blue, brilliant sky sparkling on the wheat. Long bands of yellow sunshine—a yellow butterfly resting on the road. The birds as they flew broke the light and scattered it, and shook the flakes out of their feathers. I saw, not the bird, but the sparkling weal it left along the air curving down and up, and at the ever-lengthening end, the nimbus of its wings. The air was full of flashes and skimming, and fountains of flight. We turned round and round to the crowded hilltops.

June 1st. While I was weeding the beetroot and carrots Mr. Scudamore spoke to me across the Saunders' garden and asked me to go beet-hoeing to-morrow. So I washed and scrubbed, and got ready to be out.

What a sky! It's not a sky, but one great rainbow from west to east, perfectly cloudless, perfectly clear, without moon or stars. Behind the clear one-toned hills it is flame and red, passing upward through yellow, pale ice green, and faint violet, to its own ultimate silvery blue—*its own colour* as I believe it, beyond all tinted atmosphere.

How beautiful, still and penetrating is the sense of it over us as we go to bed! How freely we move, undress and lie down, so cool-warm and soothed!

From our window I can see the slanted oak across the field dark as a yew against the glow.

The sky tingles with a million million thrilling atoms. It is eternal lightning; a thousand thousand abiding summer flashes; it is quiet rainbows and the bright voids around the evening stars. Naked we bathe our bodies in the air. Naked all things look to me, so pure and bright that all reflections are the reflections of light itself.

Looking out of the window, out and above the west, over the twilight, *I feel my naked eyes*. Space has bared them. By the window in the crystal darkness, the clothing of sight was swept from my bared and breathing eyes . . . it seemed to me afterwards lying in the grey room, that the very furniture was nude. Our skins gleamed over our shoulders and knees: our limbs had a roundness, a length, a *simplicity*—as if our ordinary nakedness had been sloughed, to reveal another purer contour, a rainbow glow of being.

2. Woke early and saw the transparent moon in the sky hanging between the east and south with its edge to earth. I'm going to hoe in a moment. The sunlight is lying across the floor on Walden and my MSS. All the small birds are singing and cheeping . . . the horizons are white. Over us is arched a great and sparkling sky, pale with heat. The insects fly with lighted bodies. Morning and evening are twin lakes with green day edging them. The sun and the early star two islands . . . Oh morning, morning, the fresh earth, the dew spattered in the wake of the first flight! I am absorbed in the beauty, the meaning, the exquisite *retentiveness*. It is as though all Nature senses and abstains, putting forth a limb at sunrise, feeling towards the day with caution and reserve. How slow the dawn; how slow to develop and dispel! How happy I am—how joyous is my heart in which the time is happening!

Later. I hoed until half past four. They gave me a bath and a cup of tea at the Court, and then I came home and got the supper and gardened.

3. To-day I went to Ross, cleaned the brasses, turned out two bedrooms. Cooked, washed up, and stayed out in the garden till half past ten, watering, Dutch hoeing, moving young plants. . . .

We went to the stream to bathe. Washed my feet at the very last in cold rainwater, and then naked into bed. Sometime in the night it was very dark and I felt I saw the stars shining.

The flowers in the field. While M—— was in the stream I lay and looked at them. Over the grasses, over and under the fibrous roots twisted among themselves, the ants crawled like little boats on choppy seas. The little wild grass vetch with single roman purple flower, the pink orchis, the daisies suppliant with ecstasy, manifold. The petals of the buttercups mirror a perfect miniature sun faithfully shining towards the western sky. It isn't just a spot of light on the surface, but a planet in the flower. The charlock blooms, the honeysuckle, the floating oxeye. The dandelion's ball of mist is seen against the sky, erect and motionless upon its hollow silver stem. In the evening light upon the wild hill, the thistles are seen veiled in diaphanous white cloud, formless yet defined, like breath in frosty weather. The purple-headed rye grass gives a sheen to the surface of the clover: there is no glitter, only a long smooth reflection to the light sky above, broken by the fierce yellow flare of the rag-wort flowers. I lay and looked and felt no wind on my bare skin. Yet all the flower heads were softly, almost unnoticeably, swaying on their stalks as if thus they breathed and were . . .

I saw, too, this evening a pair of red beetles in the act of mating in the coolness under the chrysanthemum bushes. Theirs was a wonderful colour, between terra cotta and pure coral dull, and without burnish. The male was only half as large as the female under him. All the time they waved their black antennae.

4. It's ten in the morning. Oh so hot and pale. There's a sort of exhalation round the trees. I cannot quite see through to them.

Later. I spent hours in the field to-day. And I don't think I shall make many more entries in this journal—perhaps only one. Silence. The beauty, the power, the central stillness of all life overpowers speech. Only by living can I perfectly respond. Even if I had time I couldn't write what I am at this moment thinking. The spirit calls me too far away, calls to me in a language never invented far beyond the use of 'merely.' To neither the life of thought nor the life of service do I entirely belong. . . .

All day the sun shone on the fields, the rows of plants, the weeds. The men and the flowers and the trees were the in-habitants, and the light lay under his mansion. There was no wind. The birds were silent, the farm doorways open and empty. The paths bare, the cattle and sheep alone upon the green. Once a jackdaw flew over, and the cuckoo haunted the short horizon. From where I worked the stillness went out and out to eternity.

I had my dinner alone under the hedge by the flowering elder. I was rapturously happy. I took off my shoes and felt the hot, smooth, cracking earth. Then I lay down and spread a rhubarb leaf over my head.

To-night we washed in the stream and afterwards walked together up our lane home. A blur of mosquitoes, a sunlit band, extended from an inch or two above the water to the mid-girth of the willows. In the sky a lilac tone, softening the blue, most delicately clear, a veil for the small gentle summer stars. . . . The lambs' black ears wriggling over the tops of the hedges, the gold light on the leaves draining back into the sun as it sank behind the elms. Daisies and buttercups closed and the wild parsley growing out of the grass. The light of the evening was its air: it was neither twilight nor daylight but cool faint-coloured atmosphere which seemed to fold each flower and tapering grass round with a solitary sky, a solitary universe. I saw each and all as if it were the only one . . . as if each soared alone against the glow—the gold, the white, the purple. To walk and breath, to stretch out an arm was to enjoy and be conscious of an increase in being. Every movement gave joy as it stirred the quiet air against the body. To live in every inch; *to be oneself throughout.* It has been the quietest of days. In the field the hoes tinkled, the voices glided one into another . . . one of the daughters at the farm carried home a fledgeling chaffinch which she had picked up on the road two miles away. They fed it with chopped worms and left it on the lawn. The reason for its helplessness was a deformity in growth: one wing was bare of pinions, the other fully developed. All the time it crouched and opened its great mouth to the sky. Presently they saw birds drop down and feed it—old birds which could never have known it but which were related to its need.

5. The great bee day. Just before dusk we brought the swarm home to Panbrook in a rusty tar barrel.

6. By the stream nearly all day. The blacksmith bird. The north wind began to blow, and it blew.

7. To-day

8. To-day

9. To-day. We hoed to-night.

10. The north wind was still blowing when I went out into the garden this morning. I was remembering how suddenly the birds fell silent last night, and the cattle bellowed. I had a curious dream which has filled my mind all day. In it there is a cowstall with a wooden bar running its length instead of a manger. I *see* only a portion. Is it dark over there in the corner? Or does the dream end like a map? It's a country where oxen are driven. One large beast is tied to the bar, and one of its horns has been sawn off. They all have this done to them. It's the custom here. And the young man comes and flings a sort of halter over the beast's neck. 'We shall ride fifteen miles,' he mutters. Oh! I protest: 'I don't think I *could* do that.' But we are outside. It's a flat, wet lane. I see chains of water in the ruts. . . . It happened that when we were hoeing yesterday the men were arguing over a cow losing a horn; some saying that it would never grow again and others persisting that they had known it to do so.

On the way to the field saw a moorhen tugging away over the dull yellow pond at the point of a lovely silver V. It was all that pleased me, so overcast, so cold, the sky, the trees.

We finished the beet and began the potatoes. The four men quarrelled up and down the rows:

'You're not educated . . . you don't read.' And to the oldest one: 'Who gave the laying mash to the pigs? A-ha-ha-ha! Uncle caught it that time.'

It's cold—cold. My hands have a greyish, dead tinge. And the twilight is coming. Rain whispers, and pauses. The tall fir is very dark, without a branch moving. The sheep call incessantly.

12. I've carried all my books and papers and betaken myself to the window where the sun shines on every pane. It's the only warm place in the house. I crowd into it. . . . The sun is shooting out a tremendous white light; in its heart I seem to be able, for a second, to see a dark spot of blue or purple, like the pupil of an eye. . . .

Each grass is silver, each broad bean leaf separate and distinct . . . a cock is crowing. It's early evening . . . and before going to bed I listened to the cricket. It was like the winding of a bobbin on a sewing machine. It was easy to realize' that this was no song, but a sound produced by mechanism. (Isn't the voice?) As the twilight began to shine in the sky, more and more crickets joined forces, thrilling the grasses which hid them, and lining the lane with their whirring.

13. As I went into the field by the pond, I saw a plover rise up from just in front of me, and hover, suspended, as it were in my own eyes. I heard the cry from his throat break in two, and I saw the sky through the rugged coast of his wings. Hoed with the men. From the quiet farm no glimpse of occupation; nobody at windows or doors or walking along the paths through the meadows where dreamy cattle were lying. . . . The men talked of record wheat crops.

15. The wind keeps turning the page. I'm writing on the floor in the middle of the morning. A bumble bee is banging his poor head against the wall in the corner.

How I enjoyed the evening of last night! I sat by our window looking across the field of clover. The dew was being distilled from the gathered glow of the day . . . so calm, so quiet. The hills were grey, the sky all tiny pale gold clouds, like curls: the red sun, partly veiled, hung over the clump of elms. . . .

This morning I looked out as I was dressing and saw the broad field all blotted with dew, the butterflies wavering over the hedge. It came to me slowly what was partly the meaning of morning to me. I have been conscious of it for a long time, yet I cannot put into words the acute but *diffused* desire in me to *spend* myself—to flow in all directions and meet and merge and enjoy all beautiful things. I want to be everything, to go everywhere! I thought I would go down and put my face in the dewy clover—I would walk out into space and touch the north, south, east, and west, the green which is the hair on the frame of the hills . . . feel it with my passion, love it as the sun whose great white flame curled up into the infinite sky. The very grass heads called to me; the fields were yearning, the sky reflected in earth.

And then, the morning is gone, and I have followed but one single way, been with few joys, and lo! it is over.

The intense desire to be united with Nature grows in me with the impossibility of achieving it or comprehending the longing. Rarely, for a moment, it happens: but constantly and every day I want it without ceasing. Most often and most easily it comes in the simple, tranquil work in the fields. Leisure with its boundaries only serves to define to me the difference between respite and continuous, abiding existence in life—the Life of Eternal Time, in which being, or being dispelled, my essence shall pursue the wind forever. It's my belief that the wild creatures know joy in being as we who pursue our minds ahead will never know it until our bodies, draining into the earth, end the race with the undying. . . .

17. It's the kind of evening which comes at any season. The clouds were the colour of the pigeon feathers strewn about the field. We stood between the rows of swedes and watched the flocks of sparrows hurtle their twinkling bodies into that purplish gloom behind the tall hedge. We had been hoeing our row of potatoes which are across the fields below the swedes. We went up the row passing over each other, chopping up the thistles and dodder.

23. My evening. As I went by them I touched with my finger-tips the suspended grass ears. They were like weights which my touch set swaying, heavy and white with polleny flowers; and they left a white dust on the skin. The great flat hemlock blooms smelled thick and rank. The acacia flowers fallen in the road were like sawdust. . . .

One little boy was in bed with a milk can full of cherries. The other was learning his Catechism on the broad windowsill, leaning on his elbow and rubbing the cat's tail.

I had a bath. It was lovely to be naked.

Coming up the hill I felt so tired and yet *clear*. The willow trees, the immensely tall foxgloves, the cuckoo calling over fields and fields of uncut hay.

24. Old midsummer. B—— A—— is cutting the clover. It lies in tumbled waves. Rattle—rattle. Whoa—pause—I'm doing the washing.

Wild bees. There are many different kinds but all are much larger and much more beautiful than our small drab honey-bees. They have their nests in warm, sandy banks. Mrs. Saunders told me how the children will defy them and poke out their honey with sticks. She said she has often tasted it. I've handled many wild bees and never had a sting. There was one on the parlour windowsill, squatting in a coma as though sunstricken. She was medium sized, dark brown or black with very thick glossy fur. Caked in a groove in each of her hindmost legs above the joint, was a flattish lobe of pollen, greeny grey and waxy. They were such immense loads that she looked as if she were carrying panniers, and even more like an antique paddle-steamer. I saw she was exhausted and must die, for she could hardly drag herself along. . . . So, having refreshed her with a flower into which she dug her black proboscis as if to suck its heart, I fetched a very delicate, sharp pair of curved nail scissors and sheared away the lumps as near her legs as I dared. Then I put her on the outer sill, where she began to crawl more briskly; and when I next looked she was gone.

Another bumble bee I was watching was working on a foxglove. She disappeared into the bag of the flower which began to heave and stand away from the stalk as if a goblin had got into it. The most interesting circumstance was the noise she made—a sort of dry blundering and scratching which could be heard five or six strides away.

(Note. Once, much later in the season, I heard a wild bee making a sound incomparably louder. It was rolling down the lane, close under the bank, clenched into a ball, and uttering, or making, a continuous buzzing or shrilling. It seemed as if it were in a kind of fit and gave me the impression that it was in great agony. I believed that it must be fighting with some tiny and malignant insect or parasite—but it proved to be clutching nothing. I have never seen any creature in greater distress. Also it was of a most enormous size, and barred with a thick orange bar as vivid as a tiger's gold.)

On this night we went up to B—— to watch for the badgers. I wanted to stay up, not for the badgers but because it was midsummer, and I was expecting a crisis and miracle of beauty.

It was ten o'clock, and the sky burned with a pure heatless flame over the tree tops. I could feel the dew condensing in the air, and the tang of the moonlight dawning into the brightness . . . the meadows through the trees were to the last like streaks of faint green light . . . the song of the stream seemed jubilant, as if it had heard itself and loved its sound—the only continuous one. While I was sitting there I tried to isolate its notes, and place their pitch in my imagination: but my hearing strayed from point to point, as the wide twilight made stark each stir and motion of life. . . .

At the end of the tunnel of trees the sheep roamed against the red west, feeding on a ridged bit of field. They seemed to nibble into the silence, cropping as they moved slowly across the glow. Such sky behind them! as if the whole heaven were the surface of one soft summer star, containing all its light and shining only by its purity and difference from earth. Unlike the wrinkled red of winter sundown there was nothing aged in the day's last look. As the sun passed swiftly under the world leaving the sky clear as an anemone, the waning west watched its reflection in the pregnant east, and the moon of dew felt the moon of fire behind her.

In a cottage some one shut a window. I heard the partridges wheezing—'kee-ee-click, kee-click, kwee-ee-klik.' And until nearly midnight the far commotion of the burning haymaking, settling and cooling like embers into the ashen earth. Yet there was infinitely more of silence than of sound. The wave on the stream was white like a feather; the darkness of the trees smoked upward. We stayed so breathlessly concealed in stillness and green sprays that the wild duck from the end of the reservoir mistook us for darkness and solitude, and came swimming down towards us. I saw the undulations and the breaking water moulded on their breasts; but moved . . . and M—— moved . . . and they turned back before they were anything to us but a silvery crescent of wakes and waves. It didn't matter that we never saw them or the badgers . . . so exquisite was the sky, the firm blue hills, the pause upon the climax. The light upon the moon was a yellow cloud, dim within sharp space. It was never dark even under the trees, even at midnight. But a great bow of shade spanned the topmost leaves from north to south. No stars were in it, but the sunset burning on and on, and in the east prophetic light.

I felt the sun was barely sheathed in earth. Sitting there watching the pale sparkle of space through the dark leaves and twigs, feeling the invisible dew falling through the spinney, with my eyes sometimes fixed on the dim red bank with its zoo-like caves and runs, in a calm within a calm, I drank each moment and felt no more chill or weariness than the naked eyeball feels the air. Crouched against the tree's body, in its arms, I searched for the source of the impalpable twilight. Where? where was it, the night? Where the subduing, the silence, the shadowing? The flowers in the fields felt it—the sparse golden flowers cool and closed—the quiet foxgloves, the black, pointing leaves. The sheep felt it. They thought no one was near them; I could tell it from the way they nibbled and roamed. Yet at midday the sky was no clearer.

I thought it was the earth which was night, not the sky. The form of the leaves was as drooping darkness, the scents were deeper and damper—the stealthy sounds were as bloom upon the stillness, the paths were as virgin grass. Around us the earth was become virgin again; and we were not. Only the creatures that live in her knew her, and yet did not know her. They passed over earth unconsciously free, even of liberty.

When we came away the moon was high and shining thinly over the cold grasses. Behind her, chasing her with a cloud of light, the daybreak followed. Farther and farther away from the fringed fields the moon floated . . . our glassy shadows lay on the stones in the lane. As we passed we looked up at sleeping windows and waves of pallid flowers suspended in a gentle gloom. The dense blue hills were distinct, solemn and separated, and the land all round was encircled with a russet glow like a frost ring. Then I felt the three planets of sun, moon and earth, and their inter-intelligence. This was my very midsummer hour.

27. The cat, Thomas Pusso. *When* he stretches, licks his milky chin and leaps on the windowsill (as at this moment) I know it's really morning, really evening. From my bed, or from the floor where I'm writing, I watch him, for he is suddenly the mystic he habitually is *not*. All day he's meowed, gobbled, thieved and had forty winks on the wall or under the bushes on the hot garden. Now he *knows*. Through his serene eyes he seems to gaze on irrevocable beauty. His lids are raised; and the distended eye stretches to the luminousness of evening, the sublimeness of morning. Now he lives and breathes through his eyes in the trees and the sound of the streams. With his paws curled under his broad white breast, he rests upon contemplation. Sometimes his ears twitch as if from some teasing echo of the jingling day; but only a sharp irrational noise will tempt him to turn his head.

28. Washed, cooked and watered the garden. My tudor rose unfolded to-day.

We bathed in the stream. While I was on the bank and M—— in the water, a sun ray touched me, and the shadow of a woman's body suddenly appeared behind M—— as if cast by his solid brown and white flesh.

To-night is grey and terribly sultry. I lie in bed listening to the restless, half-stifled cries of the sheep who have gathered out of the valleys on the hilltpos.

29. Opening the door in the morning I go out into the warm air unchanged all night. It's early. . . . I smell the night-scented stock, the cut clover. It's intensely still over the dewless field. The swathes are full of withered flowers.

Later. They came with the big red and blue machinery and loaded the clover. They have built the rick before the sunrise where the oat stack was last year. In this late sunlight it looks palest, bleached green, moon dried. But towards the west end the eaves are golden russet, dying to grey shadow. Mist lies over and between the trees. A quiet day is turning into night and it seems a long journey for the eye to pass over the field to the dropping sun.

I have just been out in the garden and seen a moth sipping the night-scented stock. It interested me, so that I stood a long time watching it with my little watering jug in my hand. A parched scent of clover dust was in the air, like ash instead of dew, and the cries of the sheep came softly and thickly up from the meadows . . . the moth hovered at the centre of the flowers, its body quiveringly upheld between the whirling wings, drinking as if with rapture . . . it was a delicate gauzy creature . . . and when it flew seemed almost to weave a nest of light. Yet its flight was stronger than that of the excited butterflies which is so emotional and bubble-like that when they pass out of sight one thinks of them no more.

Margaret came and told me she is going to begin to take honey this week.

Now I must water. The evening is full of large, soft tranquillity, of sound and misty echo.

July 13*th*. That was a fortnight ago. To-day M—— left home for the Navy and the earth and I look strangely on each other. This was not what I saw, this was not what I felt.

MORNING

In a certain stage of their flight, when rising from earth but still low enough to loom large in the watcher's eye, the crows take the form of a starfish. With wings stretched to the utmost extension, back slanting upward to the head, tail pointing to the ground, resting as it were on the unspent force of the first pulse of flight as a swimmer on his stroke, yet still being driven upward with all the power they can command, for a long second the birds are seen spread upon the background of sky as a starfish is razed upon the beach. For the crows and rooks rise with a sideways and upward tilt of the body, presenting as narrow an edge as they possibly can to the wind. From one angle both pointed wings, head, back and tail are all seen at once, giving a marvellous sense of life and vigour. The effort of lifting themselves fills their furthest outlines, and seems to attain for them temporarily a firmer and less sluggish being. They become taut and beautiful as sea-creatures until the wind getting under them floods them into the deeper sky, there to caw and drift on their moods. As they rise and diminish their dark-blue colour like a wet mussel shell is forgotten and they are thought of as dark brown or black birds until the next time the eye is surprised by their nearness.

This morning I startled some of them feeding where the chain harrow had grazed the ground by our wood-pile. When they saw my head over the wall they were already several feet up in the air; but it seemed a long time before they *decidedly* flew away. I saw the sunlight on their backs rousing all their colours. It cannot have been many seconds before they were out of sight but for some reason it seemed mental ages. In-decisions, hoverings seemed in all our minds, circling from one to another: and the sun, overcoming cloud for the moment, rested on us all as if for the length of our lives. The sun it was that made the scene permanent in my mind so that I see it again in every detail—the dark-blue wings and bodies in the air, the ground littered with sodden chips and sticks, the green clover growing, and the marks of the harrow swerving from the wood-pile. I couldn't express what thoughts were mine while I looked over the wall at the field, over my shoulder at the garden earth dug round the lilac tree. I believe I had none. The morning was in me; but the morning and the light are utter in themselves and have no expression but in their being. Long before we wake morning finds its way into our minds. Through our many sleeping thicknesses light reaches us before our eyelids open. Though we wait for the morning it is always there before us.

I had no thoughts. The field and the moist damp earth thought for me. The sky thought in cloud and sun, in the echoes of bird song, and the cries of ewes and lambs, in the flight and calling of plovers under the cloud shadows. The earth thought in the bright green blades of the grass weed, washed by the rain against the lumps of black soil. The trees echoing with thrushes and blackbirds, and the bush out of which flew a chaffinch, were all of them thoughts in the morning which contained all silent and articulate life.

As the chaffinch flew across the wood-pile I saw the bits of white among his feathers, and his pink breast rounded by the air. He rushed into a bush near by and from there began once more his incessant headlong phrase which pours out from his throat like a pent-up idea.

'Again, again!' sang the thrushes longingly.

'Believe it, believe!' the blackbirds called. Then they were all silent as the rain tumbled down out of the sky. But when it stopped, and the wood-pile dripped from every twig and the green bark shone, they loudly applauded as though to listen to the rain being flung to earth were the great delight of their souls. 'Again, again!' they sang, calling one another back to the beginning of the song.

Near, very near, was the bleating of the lambs, yet far away and spread out too, like a universal sound, a shrill, insect buzzing coming up from the fields, from the hills, from the dry pale patches under the elms. From the lane came the deep lazy cawing of the rooks swaying on the thin topmost branches as they lectured on law and nests. Sometimes the sun stole into the mild air, expanding it into light, blooming faintly on the clouds. Sometimes the wind sowed the rain over the land, flinging it like handfuls of grain against the window panes, dropping it with separate, minute vibrations, each striking an exquisite aural nerve, upon the shed roof and the smooth black water in the butts.

I breathed and felt the freshness mounting in me to the perfection of its meaning. Morning, morning, my veins, and the stones in the wall, my brain and spirit and the very minute lichens, are full of it. The sky is different from itself at any other time, and I am a different being from the one who went to sleep last night. There is something in me which was not there then. The same element which drives the lapwings before the wind and makes their call come over the fields as an echo of an echo of an echo, linking me to the silent horizon, has repaired the worn and injured cells of the mind. More, has put into them hope. Not old hope refreshed, but new hope, hope which until this moment did not exist in this world. It is fresh life, and vigour and promise I feel in me, not refreshed. I am so new to myself I scarcely know my limbs, strength, extent of spirit. Uncast into any mould or plan of shape, the hours ahead seem each a holiday. I linger, slowly touching, tasting, imbibing the earth and the morning.

'Again, again, again! Believe it, believe!' Such words seem to me imbedded in the bird music and in my brain. All the air is full of sound, of mild cloud, light and rain. The calling of the lambs becomes a frenzy, each scattered bleat joining the crowd of sound by the gate. The thrushes love this interrupted rain. All living things love the spark in the raindrop, the assertion of its sound. Even the stones, and the vibrant air whose life is so immense we cannot assimilate it.

This one raindrop, so darkly clear reflecting in its globule the cloud behind it; this raindrop, one among a handful clinging to the pane, was only a moment ago hurled against the glass with a hard, sharp 'rap!' I watched it collect over Garway hill, a dozen miles away, looming and glooming nearer the sun and me. Now like bubbles in ice they cling to the pane, seeming to be neither on one side nor another, but inside the glass, so instantaneously *still* are they. But slowly the weight in them drags them downward; they elongate and sag, holding by a rim of iridescent water, but dark in the middle with a clear seed of light, like a bird's eye. Then suddenly they shoot down the pane, leaving a more transparent track than glass. . . .

Ages is in the process. The imagination is suspended while each globule exists. A bloom like that on certain flowers darkens the atmosphere, makes blue the heavy grey cloud behind them.

To be alone in the morning is sweeter than concord, more sustaining than sympathy. There is something in you then which you have not planned—something which makes you breathe as you *can* breathe and which lets your movements, though full of energy, be full of leisure too. Working is as much pleasure as being idle, standing and watching takes no time out of a dwindling day. What is this strong serenity? this early instinct to be happy? Ah, why do I ask, I wonder, as I lean against the wall, since the others round me don't? I don't want an answer. Never in the eye of any wild creature have I seen the shadow of a question. When I awoke I had no appointments with the hours—my body was a wilderness which only nature had planted, and no dream was left over in my brain. I saw through the open door what seemed like a grey candle burning. The walls seemed not quite upright, not quite solid. I had not heard the cock crow nor the birds awake and yet they were singing. Light had penetrated me and yet so gently that I hardly knew it was there. While I was in my soundest sleep morning had irradiated me. I got up, and in physical imitation of a spiritual state, opened every door and window, gazed and gazed, acted the dawn with my own being. Looking down from my window into the gradually emerging grain of earth my memory became illuminated with strange, small perennial lights, as a hedgerow with pale sunlight. I saw and felt things which are buried and flower only once a year in the early spring, recollections of delicate and precious sensations. I *felt* my hand going into a bank, searching under the ivy and dead grasses, for violets. Every little hollow was like a bird's nest, lined with roots and soft hay-coloured fibres. Feathers and brown leaves, even the colour of the lane's surface I saw in that flash—and I saw the sun before it had risen.

If I were ever *collected* (as it were) from the fields, and put into a solitary prison there to be in *myself* the infinity I feel—if I had no window I could reach, I would somehow find out where the sun rose and sank, and map its course on my walls. Then, whatever my lack, I could not become callous to the morning. I should have the universe, and the feeling of the universe to give me the extension of life seeing and feeling confers. Unless one *finds out* one dies. To be paralysed is not to feel the movement of the universe. At night sometimes I am so, sitting indoors, lapsing into darkness. I sit and I ache and I long for the morning.

CONCLUSION

UNDER THE OAK TREE

ONE evening, when it was almost dark and Mother was with us children, we heard Dad shouting from the road for us to come out and look. We all ran downstairs and out of the front gate. I have an isolated and very singular memory of a great, lowering, yet very gentle star, burning at the end of our road, over the common.

'Look! it's Jupiter,' Dad said. And the mild, near light, so vast and so mysterious, awoke in us all the incomprehensible language of delight. I can see the grey rib of common now, with its charcoal smudges of furze, and feel the soft inexplicable star watching us. It was Jupiter, and its name was a shout. It was so wonderful that it had made Dad call us. The sight of it *belonged to me*: it fitted in with other experiences either absolutely perfect in their exquisite happiness, or the exact reverse.

We lived in what was then a country suburb. The best walks were over the commons along bracken-walled paths which smelled of bruised greenery. Joy went along with me—all was right, until, as always, the path ended in a wide main road. Then instead of being in some beautiful eternal 'out of doors' I found myself in the 'neighbourhood' again. The 'neighbours,' the 'neighbourhood,' was always asserting itself over something wild and beautiful, something outside houses, roads and carefully controlled gardens.

Like many children I knew what it was to be haunted by the longing to be wild, to escape not so much from having to obey, as from the obedient world. In certain places, touching certain things, by smell and by subtler sensing, I succeeded. These places and things I loved. One was a young sycamore which was growing in our front garden close by the fence. I cannot describe my sensations when I put my hands round its slender smooth trunk, except by saying that they were the exact opposite of those I experienced when the paths ended. Existence, both real and imaginative, was ranged into a curious pattern of for and against. Jupiter, the sycamore, our never used backgate, bolted with bramble sprays. were all Fors. So were all the wild flowers, particularly the dry, delicate harebells: and the peacock butterflies in the gravel pit, the sour wood strawberries, the sight of ivy and winter berries, the mud and mist of the autumnal fields. Among the Againsts was our grandfather's garden, which was strange, because it was much deeper in the country than our own and had a field on one side where cattle and horses grazed. I think that first profound yearning must have been an instinctive one—for earth but not only for earth. Rather for happiness in earth. Earth could be spoiled by humans, even innocent grass and heavenly sky could be distorted by the unlovable presence as when a strict, tart-spoken friend of my mother's took us out one afternoon, and supervised us while she sewed in the very spot over which the magnificent star had appeared on that remarkable night. Oh how well I remember the dreariness! the warm evening smell of the common which seemed to have been *used* over and over again, as we sat breathing it! Those two events, Dad calling us out in the dark, and the spectacled old lady seated sewing in a dell, were the very antithesis of each other, and represent oppositely what was in my mind during early childhood. My mind then, as now, was in my body. Its emotions were not as concrete as writing makes them; but it is impossible to describe them otherwise because at the time consciousness could do no more than materialize itself in trees and flowers and a certain *remoteness* which was limited in a suburb. Childhood stops, is annihilated. But the things in childhood which were not childish are permanent. Their colours are fixed in the character, like the prism in the adult eye. As the infant blue dissolves over grey and green, yet underneath remains the same organ, with the same selective vision, my self endures as it was in those days.

In the selection made by vision in the past lies the true solution of our being. Visions in childhood have childish form but they are not childish in themselves. By visions I mean quite ordinary things which possessed for some reason extraordinary powers. Everything happened to me when I was a child, and though all the vestiges of my childhood are gone out of the world, what was deepest in me then is my depth still. Still the earth and sky make their living, close, yet far distant appeal to my being. A summons sounds under my feet, by my hand, in the ear and eye which seem forever pressed against the air, to catch that murmur of sight, that vision of sound, whose first thrilling even when I was so young seemed to come over immeasurable time and distance. I still have those startling moments, memories from the first instant, which bring through my physical body a spiritual awareness indescribable. Sometimes with a touch they are over: sometimes days cannot contain them. All that I have learned since, that is valuable, is where I may find them. In the same way as when I was little some places are right and others wrong—worse than wrong, hideously adverse to me, persistently awry, as if I were going against my natural instincts by being in them. Of these places I could not write. I don't understand them, or why they exist. I have found them usually near towns, but also where there seems to be nothing lovely missing except my own ease. But as this autobiography is the record of my gravest (that is happiest) inner existence, I shall end it with a description of the place where I feel I have reached my uttermost growth. Its meaning to me is the same as the soft touch of the star a long time ago, and it smells through and through of the same old smell as the first turf I lay on—the same old primitive smell of earth's hide.

It is under an oak tree where the short grass is the dry colour of a hare's skin, yet shot with silky golden moss, and bound with the roots of wild flowers. Being there is to be in the open yet in a sort of slightly hollow room, walled on three sides by bushes and the oak's trunk, on the fourth by the hill's slope up to the southern sun. Its roof is unceiled, tiled with blue or grey sky scaffolded with immense horizontal beams the tree throws out a little more than my height from the ground at the ends. What gives it an enchantment that no room ever had, even in childhood, is that it is furnished with ancient green ant humps, and that the pattern under your feet changes with the fall of leaves or the growth of flowers. I cannot express the feeling of shelter and solitude, of thoughts not too complicated but too simple for words, which come to me there, as bending by chance to pick up a stick, my fingers sweep the dry softness, or touch a purple blackberry leaf where the single dark spray starts out of the ground. It is all so responsive, yet so peaceful—I am stimulated to a grave contentment. For nobody ever is there, and the real inhabitants, after hesitating a moment, take no notice of the one who has sat down in their midst. This sweet, still room scented dryly of oak leaves and bracken, belongs to the rabbits and the small chippy noted birds whose short flights flutter the bushes. Many wrens are there, and tom-tits and finches. Pigeons strike the tree roofs; deep in the hazel and alder the magpies rattle; the woodpecker breaks away as if forever, and from the domed spaces all around I hear the plovers' and partridges' call.

All these sights and sounds, heard so often, bring fresh thoughts into my existence. The most trivial detail does so, for the atmosphere is as a mind opening itself to mine. I see the branches over me, and I visualize the hidden roots underneath, as the tree inverted. No sheep are ever pastured on this bit of wild land, perhaps because they could so easily fall into the stream's deep gully, and lie there on their backs till they died. But sometimes three ponies graze there and then horse hairs stick to the bark. I have watched these hairs floating out from the tiny excrescence which holds them, until truly they seemed wonderful, with the wonder that waits for everything in creation. A leaf, floating down is a communication; it has come out of the sap, has gone from the tree to the earth, touching with its tiny point of life the infinity of my universe. I cannot name nor define its journey, but only feel it truly for its meaning.

My oak tree stands in eternal time; and when I am by it I too exist in that. It takes just long enough for me to reach it from home, for me to begin to think. When my saw got blunt and had to go to be sharpened and set, I came nearly every day to pick up wood. The blacksmith was slow and my sticking went on over many weeks. Often before I used to go and sit and lie under it, leaning my shoulder against its trunk, learning by heart the little bay of hard red ground, the kidney coloured fungus, all the minutiae of grass blade, moss and leaf . . . learning so well and so unconsciously that I can call them up at any time as easily and distinctly as the pattern of my hearth rug at home. To *need* the wood—to have to go for part of your simplest existence out of doors, is to regain the primitive ground lost when some began to carry and others to receive at the door. Our necessities have a living holiness which brings health: they should not become relics, vegetable-like bones delivered out of the unknown darkness.

I don't always go to the tree for something that I can put in a sack however. Often and often walking up and down between the coppice and the stile, by looking into the wide field I have cleared my soul of pain, and seen my true beliefs acting vividly and swiftly around me in the creatures that glanced aside as I passed. In the early September morning I saw the stubble partly cleared, lying around the harvest's brown and misty camp, under skies of opal grey. The loaded wagons had swept the hedge and crooked straws were hanging broken over the sloe twigs. I seemed to be there without a motive, as though I expected my intention to be waiting. As the sun rose, it was for that I had come, to see the still yellow east twinkle with my movements, behind the leaves. Walking over the field made the distant trees appear to dance across the light . . . especially when I stumbled in the cuts the huge wheels had made on the turn. Here the wagon had stood, and here a cobweb stretched over a hoof print. The ground was churned and the stubbles were crushed into the damp earth . . . in me, invisibly I saw the horses, their quarters black and clotted with sweat, wrinkling as they pulled. Then I felt the shiver of effort in my own muscles.

When I am at home my eye catches only oblique gleams of the life about me. I see heaven and earth as it were with the corner of my eye, protruding on a busy day which in the wholest sense is nothing to me. The gleam, the lighted corner, the blackbird who flies past the door while I work, are more to me than the humanness which anchors my feet to the floor. But by the oak tree, lying under it, or walking slowly around it, I look out truly, from the centre, the very core of sight, and am myself behind my eye. It is impossible then to tire: the brain ceases to entangle the body in its multiple orders: the body moves completely, as if it wished to reach the end of each stride: and the mind does not run ahead drawing one after it through vistas of jobs to be done, conscious of substance only as obstacles which abrade. All the house trivialities, the constant washing of cloth and flesh and stone, the gardening, darning, fire lighting and wood chopping, which make one get so hot in order to keep warm, all those dissipations of opportunity are forgotten, and the things that I cursed and hit myself against become once more and rightly inhabitants related to me by a most delicate and beautiful sense of contrast.

Such is the power of life over me then that I lose language and think only by being. Once I remember trying to write a letter to M——. But the stems that touched my hands, the ant hills, the crickets that jerked, and the silent clouds, had my mind in them. I could not write: I could not concentrate, for my being was in everything. The ripening berries were more real than anything I could say. How well I remember those berries!— ropes of them, glossy red and yellow in their dark-green leaves, looped and hanging over the bushes. I can hear the grasshopper's chika-chika-chee now; the magpie's rattle in miniature, a dry shingly sound out of the baked ground. I lay there on the flattened moss, pinned to the earth by a pen through the hand.

The oak tree stands in a narrow hazel and alder coppice which hides the dark, rocky gully of a tiny stream. The turf smells tiny pale yellow flowers I love bloomed among the fading grass. A buttercup too, and a knot of pale speedwells coaxed to look at the slow sun once more. Over the stream under the south bank a half ring of pure white horse mushrooms. Near us huge toadstools turned up all round like coolies' hats. Even the gnats I can remember hovering up and down in the shade, and a rabbit jumping off a molehill.

It was all of it, what I cannot tell . . . but more to us than our own individual existence. We could know together the thought that was not ours as we could never share our own; perhaps because speech cannot ever express such simplicity, perhaps because the sense of life in people is so delicate and vulnerable that communication breaks it.

So delicate! the separate life that moved my arm over the grass, that sent my glance upward. I looked at the sun, and my eye was shut with pain: the speedwell looked and its unseeing eye opened, feeling the light through its wan blue, with humble, happy joy.

Ah, I cannot lie in the sun as those merry bullocks do. My brain, distinct from my state, tugs ahead. So powerful is the irresponsible human brain, the idiot power that we die in the battle against it: life burns low and vigour wanes. If we could only call ourselves alive! Instead of boasting that we can bear privation, if we would only say that we can endure delight, satisfaction, peace! So faint is the life in my body that it can hardly feel the pulse: it is lapse and in unconsciousness until it is roused by contact and renewed by deep physical reflection.

The iridescent town in its mother o' pearl mist, how often have I looked at it as at an opposite, yet feeling that an easier being in me might belong to it! No wonder that it seems unsubstantial in its webbing of sun squares and pale industrial smoke—for what it seems it is—a life dreamed over a foundation of beautiful, intellectual machinery. For me it is too easy to exist in a town. I feel paralysed in my brain, listlessly happy, and immune. But even then the message will reach me in the voices of the birds which sing in its crocus glades from the branches of some tarnished silver birch. The long sight of sky over roofs, the red country sun, the tang of a flock in a park, cries awaken to the one great thinking physical life, pervasive, all owning, which no stone forehead can deflect forever.

I often remember the town as I relax against the earth, and see the sunlight low among the hazel boles. Life which was weak in me when I lived there from lack of use, is nearly as weak now because my body is too hurried to think and to feel. Life is low in me: nature is a broken flame. How vital to walk and lie here under the oak, to be rested and renewed by the sight of its strength. To see things *being* . . . that is a true and firm delight, for with every leaf one reaffirms one's own existence. I write as if my body were fragile and tired. No, I am strong. I was always hard and thin, and work in the fields has developed my latent powers. My legs, my arms and back have solid muscles—it is pleasure to move them. What is weak in me is the force that makes force think: it is the natural sense of happy consciousness which lapses. That sense I call life; it is life in me, and I believe in all organisms, but in us adult humans it is only intermittent.

I am sure of one thing. And that is health. Health alone gives me some of my movements, and health sends out my sympathies. When once I saw the stoat dancing, and the viper rippling with ecstasy at the caress of the summer sun, then all over me I felt the physical echo of their joyous perfection. And watching the sunny horses tugging across the stubble field, I felt the same kind of extended well-being. The play of their muscles seemed to stimulate my own, their strength and exertion expanded me. Watching animals, flowers and leaves, and the human body, one learns to live in the eye. One learns that beauty is *never isolated*, but always related, and never ended.

It is in February that I am writing this. To-day, walking to the stile, I stopped for a little while under the oak tree. Winter gales had scattered and hidden the red-brown leaves. Crinkled and brittle, they showed here and there in the bleached grass, astonishingly vivid still. Bits of rotten branches and grey, freckled twigs lay on the ground: looking up I saw them hooked in the tree, balancing by the forks and turned downwards like diviners' rods.

As I stood there I felt some instrument in my breast throbbed to the earth. Looking up, it acknowledged the sky.

The sky and the earth were haunting in their continuity and profound peace. It was as quiet a day as when M—— and I lay there with the waning land around us.

The clouds were the constant images of peace, the hills resounded with space and spacious song. Nearby the wrens went neatly from bush to bush without a note, but the grey light under the sky swarmed with singing larks.

As I stepped the dead leaves hissed and crunched, the self-possessed birds twinkled over the brown bracken. The chaffinch sang his hasty tune, the partridges sent out their indescribable call, and some people laughing, went strolling through the meadow with their dogs. Over the stream and fields and through the distant willows came the shouting of the children running down the lane from school. Walking between the oak tree and the stile, I thought of death, as I do every day and every hour. Not death with its kneeling, and service, and decay; but of short corruption to cleanness, and the white bone in its starry beauty on the turf.

As in childhood instinct told me that there were paths which didn't end before one was tired, so now it tells me that there is a path which doesn't weary. Leaning on the stile, looking up into the impenetrable openness of the sky, picking up and hoarding the yellow ivy leaves for delight in my hand, I had a wonderful sense of solitude stored with happiness. Then I knew that bitter loneliness is not fields of sky and hills of grass. I knew it when I was a child, then I was not sure, and now I am again certain that the earth forever innocent is forever my companion.

Being a child is the most important thing that ever happens to us. It is the essential proportion in a whole life; its truth recognized is a star regained.

I was alone under the oak tree. I am alone to-night when

from the porch I can see the complete darkness that lies under and behind the white constellations. Yet I am not lonely. By letting my mind lean towards them I can feel the touch of their light, the meaning of their presence with my own.

I am not lonely. I should only be lonely if I happened alone, if I existed alone, if I had to make myself breathe. If I had created myself and must decide for myself when to die, *then* I should be lonely, and should not ask myself why I didn't envy the strolling people their laughter, the children out of school their childhood. I don't envy them because on earth I find myself in everything, because in view of death we are all the same age.

like fur. A piece of it cut out, or a pad of moss held in the hands, would bring an infinity of ideas. It is made of flower roots: buttercups, thyme, charlock, lady's slipper, speedwell—all the exquisite dots of pure colour which the sun can shine on. As a *piece of sight* it is as full of suggestion, of intimacy, as the starry sky: the intimacy that is not near, save to the mind; the suggestion that appeals to the infinite in us. So poignant is the message it should pierce all over wrappings! Beautiful is the detail, and never tiring: peaceful and speaking to the eye, suggestive, infinitely eloquent. In the high hills where earth is ghostly, where her strength is like gossamer, there is an immortal suggestion of an answer. Vision-like, thought-like the hills and mountains seem: to look at them is to believe that an earth so dreamed may be solved by an idea. But perhaps the secret interpretation is to be found in the near, the small and solid; in the pad of turf and weeds, in the physical being which functions in creation.

Looking at this turf on an autumn or winter day when the growth has shrunk I see only a dense mass of dunnish brown. But when the sun smiles on it for a few seconds, however palely, what is discovered? Emerald grass blades the more vivid for their rarity: tall silver stems, sketched by the light, which as it mildly penetrates, makes the coppice a wilderness of broken things. And when the sleet falls hissing, and when frost covers the ground with rime, the buttercup leaves become a pure blue-green, and lie as flat as if stitched to the grey, cold hollows.

Questions which I cannot forget come to me here under the tree. They come out of the leaves, dead and withered on the ground, with a fresh vital call: out of the rind of the tree, and the green southern slope where the bullocks feed in springtime. They come in such simplicity as the clouds, and the bees which seem only alive for a moment in my hearing, so fast are they gone past my ear. They occur simply, but it is not easy to define what they are. Are questions part of being human; and is being human different from being nature? Watching the animals, the leaves which spin singly in the tree sometimes, I ask, is there a *human* nature and a universal nature? I cannot believe that differences divide—I cannot be certain even that differences really exist, unless Nature *is* differences. But why 'human nature'? I hear nothing of oak nature and ivy nature, I think, as my eye rests on the beautiful ripe yellow leaves the evergreen is shedding from a nearby elm trunk.

Shouldn't I be sad resting here if I believed that I didn't form part of universal creation in the same way as all things? Ah, I am sad, for sometimes I feel there *is* a gulf, when I meet the innocent, wild, self-contained eye of bird and beast. Must I die apart? Then in my heart invisibly a world has ended. No, I believe. I believe all creation, all life whatever to be a oneness, and then once more thought and happiness sweep through all my senses as the sunlight sweeps through the tree—happiness rounds my body; my joy is grave, profound, my grief is only an instinctive ejaculation of the heart.

To think makes me completely happy . . . to think with my senses and my soul. All day I have harassed myself with senseless bustling: it was as if a high gale rattled my bones. I have moved unconsciously and tired myself before I knew that I was awake. There was no *time*—a lie, there was time, sharp, admonitory. Time: but now I am in Eternal Time, as a child, as the oak tree. Eternal time which is immortality in life. Stones are in it, and animals, and some superbly conceived buildings to which man and earth have given their ideals . . . possibly all things whose simple character has not been bereft from them by the uses they are put to. The sun smiles on the old stones, cathedral or rough wall round a field, and whether they are interwoven with the flight of birds, or simply a long mound, dry and loose as a shingle shelf, their pores expand, and they respond with an airy bloom and colour harmony. Which of us cannot remember an ivy tendril swaying, the shadow of a bramble spray, grass, a small creeping bird, and felt *seeing* the memory, *there* was their own land, their own country? So astonishing is the spirit of life and truth, that it has excluded not the least thing from its soul.

The oak tree grows on the slope down to a tiny stream, which flows through a dark and deep channel of red sandstone. In summer the trickle is clothed in a loose garment of green. In winter the shadows of its own branches are bound around the oak's trunk like ropes, when the low sun hangs southward. On warm spring days in February and March I can sit comfortably on the north-western side where there is a flat place in the bank. There, with my back against the trunk, I can watch the stream coming down its stairs of rock. It is a very little stream, wrapped in its portentous folds, a runlet of clear topaz water, which sings like a wren. It forms pools and then glides away, the spirit water hiding under its own white light. In flood times it can fill to the green lichen's brim, its capacity, and then the hart's-tongue laps it: each flat rock is a worn threshold, smoothed by its perpetual entrance. Then its merry sound intensifies the silence which broods around and over it, as the whirring wings intensify the leaflessness of the twigs. Even in spate it is only a leap across; but it joins a larger brook after running under a stone slab like a dairy shelf, which is its only bridge. Nearby is a well of purest water. Of this spot a farmer told me a horrible story about two jealous girls which happened when he was a boy. One waylaid the other as a ghost when she was going home in the dark. The terrified victim, mad with horror, shrieking and plunging in darkness, somehow communicated her panic to the other: and the end was nearly death, for hater and hated, after tearing the clothes off their bodies on the thorns, fell senseless into the gully. 'And a terrible job we had to get them out,' said he . . . 'alive . . .'

In summer all the water that comes down could easily be piped in a fair sized land drain. The pleated stones are dry and against the green shade the sun motes and mosquitoes float in airy gold. The water in the pools is like thinnest glass: it cannot sweep away the sand, and when I bath I must splash and dabble like the birds, feeling the grit grinding minutely into my skin. A switch of bracken wets my back and shoulders. Its green smell, released by the dipping, makes it a sweet, stimulating sponge. So high are the banks, so complete the hiding under net upon net of flat hazel leaves, that I have washed there, naked, while men were chopping up an elm trunk in the meadow overhanging. When I think of that now there comes back to me the feeling of shadow on bare flesh, and the way the silence shook at each axe blow. Every thing seemed too close for *sound*: it was movement one noticed—even the leaves shaking, and the shock in the meadow's foundation. No sound and yet all the earth and the bits of sky—all, the senses humming unheard harmony . . . call it God . . . call it the music of the living world . . . eternal animation . . . any name, all that mattered to me was that it was there.

> All things come to me
> through ear and heart and hand
> the shadow through the tree,
> the water through the land.
>
> Let my hand be clear,
> shadow, be my heart;
> let music be my ear
> and listening, my art.

Most of all I want to remember M—— with me under the oak tree. It was in the autumn. I want to remember the red bracken fronds, the ladybird creeping into a fold of my coat, the acorn cups. M—— lying on his side, propped on an elbow: most of all the tree itself, with the branches crossing, and then crossing again beyond, and again and again until there was the sky with its mild scattering of cloud. The edgeless sunlight dawned into the air, making transparent gold of the leaves. Now and again one fell slowly or spun in the breeze up among the great limbs, one leaf conspicuous in that column and colony of leaves.

We crumbled the dry Indian red bracken in our hands. We touched the fallen leaves, the acorns in their cups. The bees hummed in the ivy flowers, gathering their last harvest. The